Cambric

C000263057

Elements ir

edited by
James R. Lewis
Wuhan University
Margo Kitts
Hawai'i Pacific University

RELIGIOUS NATIONALISM IN CONTEMPORARY SOUTH ASIA

Andrea Malji
Hawai'i Pacific University

CAMBRIDGE
UNIVERSITY PRESS

CAMBRIDGE
UNIVERSITY PRESS

University Printing House, Cambridge CB2 8BS, United Kingdom

One Liberty Plaza, 20th Floor, New York, NY 10006, USA

477 Williamstown Road, Port Melbourne, VIC 3207, Australia

314–321, 3rd Floor, Plot 3, Splendor Forum, Jasola District Centre, New Delhi – 110025, India

103 Penang Road, #05–06/07, Visioncrest Commercial, Singapore 238467

Cambridge University Press is part of the University of Cambridge.

It furthers the University's mission by disseminating knowledge in the pursuit of education, learning, and research at the highest international levels of excellence.

www.cambridge.org
Information on this title: www.cambridge.org/9781108825672
DOI: 10.1017/9781108919050

First published 2022

A catalogue record for this publication is available from the British Library.

ISBN 978-1-108-82567-2 Paperback
ISSN 2397-9496 (online)
ISSN 2514-3786 (print)

Religious Nationalism in Contemporary South Asia

Elements in Religion and Violence

DOI: 10.1017/9781108919050
First published online: August 2022

Andrea Malji

Hawai'i Pacific University

Author for correspondence: Andrea Malji, amalji@hpu.edu

ABSTRACT: This Element explores religious nationalism in Buddhism, Hinduism, Islam, and Sikhism and how it manifests in India, Pakistan, and Sri Lanka. At the core, nationalists contend that the continuation of their group is threatened by some other group. Many of these fears are rooted in the colonial experience and have been exacerbated in the modern era. For the Hindu and Buddhist nationalists explored in this Element, the predominant source of fear is the Muslim minority and its secular allies. For Sikhs, a minority within India, the fear is primarily of the state. For Muslims in Pakistan, the fear is more dynamic and comprises secularists and minority sects, including Shias and Ahmadis. In all instances, the groups fear that their ability to practice and express their religion is under immediate threat. Additionally, Hindu, Buddhist, and Muslim nationalists wish for the state to adopt or promote their religious ideology.

KEYWORDS: religious nationalism, Hindu nationalism, Buddhist nationalism, Sikh nationalism, Islamic nationalism

ISBNs: 9781108825672 (PB), 9781108919050 (OC)
ISSNs: 2397-9496 (online), 2514-3786 (print)

Contents

Background and Introduction

This Element explores nationalism in the religious traditions of Buddhism, Hinduism, Islam, and Sikhism and how it manifests in India, Pakistan, and Sri Lanka. At the core, nationalists contend that the continuation of their group is threatened by some other group. Many of these fears are rooted in the colonial experience and have been exacerbated in the modern era. For the Hindu and Buddhist nationalists examined in this Element, the predominant source of fear is the Muslim minority and its secular and leftist allies. For Sikhs, a minority within India, the fear is primarily of the state. For Muslims in Pakistan, the fear is more dynamic and includes secularists and minority sects such as Shias, Ahmadis, and Sufis. In all instances, the groups fear that their ability to practice and express their religion in the manner they deem appropriate is under immediate threat. Additionally, Hindu, Buddhist, and Muslim nationalists wish for the state to adopt or promote their religious ideology.

Why It Matters

As of 2021, the countries of India, Pakistan, and Sri Lanka all have some democratic features with competitive political parties and elections. However, each country has also experienced concerning democratic backsliding in the past five years (Freedom House 2021a, 2021b, 2021c). This is part of a broader global trend of democratic backsliding and the increased popularity of nationalist parties around the world. Because Hindus, Buddhists, and Muslims make up the largest percent of their respective countries, it has become an effective electoral strategy to appeal to the dominant group while ignoring, even demonizing, minority religions or sects. Although Sikh nationalism has been unique compared to Hindu and Buddhist nationalism in this respect, Sikh political leaders have used a similar strategy at the local level, leading to local success for the Akali Dal party in Punjab. While these cases all have unique features, they also help provide greater understanding about the development and impact of nationalism within a regional and global context.

Nationalism in the twenty-first century is often accompanied by polarization and the threat of violence. Haggard and Kaufman (2021) find that polarization is a particularly strong threat to vulnerable democracies. When the electorate and its leaders are increasingly polarized, the opposition, particularly minorities, goes from being a nonthreatening group with different ideologies to one that is an enemy and opposed to the interests of the nation. Once the electorate accepts that the opposition is a threat to the identity of the country, violence becomes increasingly tolerable. Thus with the rise in nationalism comes the twin threats of democratic backsliding and violence, both of which have been pronounced in the cases explored in this Element.

India, the world's largest democracy, has experienced significant democratic backsliding over the past decade. In 2021, Freedom House, the key agency measuring democracy around the world, made the notable downgrade of India from "free" to "partly free." Freedom House is a global report created by nearly two hundred analysts and advisors who are experts from academia, think tanks, and human rights committees. Each year, the "Freedom in the World" measures political rights and civil liberties among several categories, including political process, political pluralism and participation, functioning of government, freedom of expression and belief, associational and organizational rights, rule of law, and personal autonomy and individual rights. Freedom House cited Narendra Modi and the Hindu Nationalist Bharatiya Janata Party's (BJP) "discriminatory policies and increased violence affecting the Muslim population" in addition to the "crackdown on expressions of dissent by the media, academics, civil society groups, and protesters" as the reason for the decline (Freedom House 2021a). According to their report, journalists, nongovernmental organizations (NGOs), and critics of the government continue to be targeted and arrested despite a constitutional guarantee of their protection. India has officially rejected these classifications, saying they are "misleading, incorrect and misplaced" (*Hindustan Times* 2022).

Pakistan has not been considered "free" based on Freedom House's criteria, but its "partly free" status has continued to decline toward "not free" over the past five years due to the military's "enormous influence over security and other policy issues" and its intimidation of the media and "impunity for indiscriminate or extralegal use of force" (Freedom House 2021b). The military and thus the state have become increasingly supportive of an expanding role of Islam within the state at the expense of minorities, including non-Sunni Muslims. Freedom House also cited the ongoing attacks on religious minorities and political opponents by Islamist militants as a concerning cause of democratic erosion. Pakistan's increasing support of the Taliban in Afghanistan is another notable area of concern and demonstrates its ongoing proximity to religious extremism within the region.

Although Sri Lanka has experienced democratic improvements since the 2015 election of Maithripala Sirisena, it has remained "partly free" due to the lack of reconciliation efforts with its minority Hindu Tamil population since the end of the civil war. The increasing power of the executive branch and the Rajapaksa family is another cited concern. Freedom House noted that since the 2019 and 2020 elections of the Rajapaksa brothers as prime minister and president, the state has rolled back accountability mechanisms, particularly of human rights violations that previously occurred under the Rajapaksa regime during the civil war. The 2021 report noted that members of the Buddhist clergy frequently pressure the government to pursue certain policies, particularly those that expand Buddhist influence in areas with higher concentrations of Hindus or Muslims. Although religious nationalism has an established history in Sri Lanka, it is becoming increasingly merged with the Rajapaksa political dynasty within the country.

The ongoing risks of violence due to religious nationalism must also be emphasized. When combined with ongoing democratic backsliding, violence provides the opportunity for the state to further restrict citizens' rights, particularly critics and minorities. Over the past decade, India has experienced escalating incidents of violence targeted at journalists, government critics, and religious minorities. In 2020, several states in India, including India's largest state, Uttar Pradesh, passed laws preventing "forced religious conversions" aimed at preventing so-called love jihad, an alleged coerced marriage of a Muslim man to a Hindu woman (Malji and Raza 2021). These laws resulted in the arrest of several interreligious couples from 2020 onward (Malji and Raza 2021). The Committee to Protect Journalists (CPJ) also noted that in 2021, India experienced a record year of violence targeting journalists. Four journalists were murdered for their work and seven were jailed (CPJ 2021).

In Pakistan, Islamist attacks have had a substantial impact on civilians, particularly religious minorities. According to the Global Terrorism Database, from 2005 to 2015, terrorist attacks increased dramatically, with a record 2,215 attacks in 2013. Attacks in Pakistan began to decline by 2016, but Pakistan still experienced 864 terrorist attacks that year, committed mostly by Islamist groups.[1] Many of these attacks targeted religious minorities. For example, a 2017 attack on the Lal Shahbaz Qalandar Sufi Shrine in Sindh Pakistan killed 90 people and injured 350 more and a November 2016 attack in Balochistan at the Sufi Shah Noorani shrine killed 52 people and injured more than 100. A year earlier, in January 2015, a suicide attack occurred at a Shia mosque in the province of Sindh, killing 61 people and injuring 46 others. In 2013, twin suicide bombings targeted at a church in Peshawar killed 127. While the state has at times attempted to promote counterterrorism efforts in areas of concern, it has repeatedly failed to protect its religious minorities and continues to provide logistical support to Islamic extremist groups, including the Afghan Taliban.

Most of Sri Lanka's postindependence era has been defined by ethnic violence. While much of this violence was spurred by the state-led exclusionary policies of Sinhalese Buddhists, the violent response by the Liberation Tamil Tigers Eelam (LTTE) helped empower Buddhist nationalists. Since the end of the civil war in 2009, new Buddhist nationalist organizations such as the Bodu Bala Sena (BBS) have grown in strength and aimed incendiary speeches at Muslim and Hindu minorities that have led to communal riots, relocation of Hindu and Muslim holy sites, and resettlement of Buddhists in Hindu- and Muslim-majority areas (Devotta 2018). While violence in Sri Lanka has dramatically declined since 2009, the government's Buddhist nationalist policies threaten to rekindle communal violence.

Finally, COVID-19 has stressed the economic, social, and political systems of even the most developed countries. In South Asia, COVID policies and responses have divided along familiar communal lines. In India, at the start of the pandemic, the Muslim group Tablighi Jamaat was accused of bringing COVID into the country and spreading it as a bioweapon (Israelsen and Malji 2021). Journalists and critics of the government have also been

---

[1] The Global Terrorism Database data are available at start.umd.edu.

targeted. For example, one journalist who criticized the Gujarat government's coronavirus response was charged under the Sedition Law and the Disaster Management Act (CPJ 2021). In Pakistan, several prominent conservative imams told Muslims to ignore any pandemic-related restrictions and attend prayers, with many attacking police officers who attempted to enforce restrictions (Freedom House 2021b). In Sri Lanka, the government initially imposed mandatory cremations for victims of COVID-19, a practice that is explicitly forbidden in Islam (Malji and Amarasingam 2021). Despite reassurances by the World Health Organization that cremation was unnecessary, the government of Sri Lanka continued the policy for nearly nine months, further marginalizing and enraging much of the Muslim community.

What Is Covered in This Element?

Religious nationalism in Sikhism, Hinduism, Buddhism, and Islam are analyzed in this Element and represent a broad cross-section of the diverse ways nationalism manifests in the region. Buddhist and Hindu nationalism share many similarities in the framing of their concerns about the Muslim minority population. Both fear a demographic shift that will potentially put them as the minority religion within the next generation or two. Hindu and Buddhist nationalists have also closely aligned with the ruling parties in India and Sri Lanka, so examining their roles vis-à-vis the state makes analytical sense. This fear has been increasingly manufactured through media and social media (particularly Twitter, Facebook, and WhatsApp) narratives emphasizing an immediate threat and challenging traditionally liberal/progressive culture (Udupa 2018).

Islamic nationalists in Pakistan do not have the same population dynamics as India and Sri Lanka. Muslims constitute 95–98 percent of Pakistan's population and 80–90 percent of Pakistan's Muslims are Sunni.[2] Sectarianism is thus the nature of nationalism in Pakistan, and the

---

[2] The exact percentages of Sunnis and Shias are not clear since Pakistan estimates do not distinguish between sects. While many estimates suggest Shias may constitute 10–15 percent of the population, a 2012 Pew Research Center survey found only 6 percent of Pakistani Muslims were Shia.

10–20 percent belonging to minority sects are the primary target of Muslim nationalists. However, non-Sunni Muslims are not generally framed as a demographic threat in Pakistan.[3] Instead, Muslim minorities such as the Sufi, Shia, and Ahmadi are presented as blasphemous or, in the case of the Ahmadis, not even Muslim. Progressive and moderate Muslims, including within civilian leadership, have also been a frequent target.

Finally, although this Element is entitled *Religious Nationalism in South Asia*, not all South Asian countries are included in the analysis. India, Sri Lanka, and Pakistan are the only three countries examined. These countries were selected for a few key reasons. First, as India and Pakistan are both nuclear powers, the impact of nationalism in those two countries is politically salient. The history of conflict and instability between the two threatens to escalate tensions to a high level, one with the potential for the use of nuclear weapons. Further, with the collapse of the US-backed Afghan government in August 2021 and the return of the Taliban, Pakistan's embrace of Islamic nationalism and Taliban-friendly policies may promote destabilization in the region and have a global impact. Finally, Sri Lanka provides the strongest example of Buddhist nationalism within the region. As the only Theravada Buddhist country in the region besides Bhutan, Sri Lanka allows the reader to see many of the parallels between Buddhist nationalism in Sri Lanka and Hindu nationalism in India. In fact, despite stark religious differences among the cases covered in this Element, there are key commonalties among their religious nationalisms.

There is widespread academic disagreement over what countries constitute South Asia. While India, Nepal, Bangladesh, and Sri Lanka are almost always included in the region (see Figure 1), there is dispute about the inclusion of Afghanistan, Myanmar, and the Maldives. Afghanistan and Pakistan are often grouped with Central Asia or even the Middle East. Events in Afghanistan are intricately linked to developments in Pakistan

---

[3] This is not to say non-Muslim minorities are not persecuted, as the blasphemy laws and targeting of the Christian, Hindu, and Sikh communities demonstrate. Instead, religious minorities are not framed as the same type of demographic threat they are portrayed as in India and Sri Lanka.

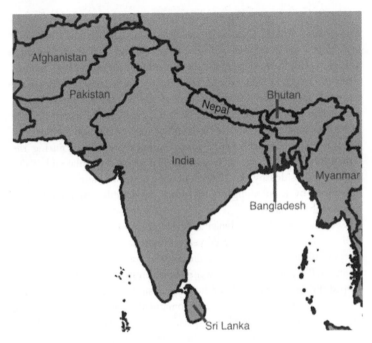

Figure 1 Map of South Asia

and vice versa. Myanmar, despite formerly being part of the British Raj, is popularly labeled as a Southeast Asian country and is a member of the Association of Southeast Asian Countries (ASEAN). Buddhist nationalism in Myanmar has grown considerably in the past two decades and shares many similarities with the movement in Sri Lanka. The 2021 coup in Myanmar provides a concerning example of the potential of a military-backed junta that frequently aligns with religious extremist Buddhist organizations such as the Ma Ba Tha. Therefore, this Element provides only a brief insight into a much larger regional dynamic that should be explored further in expanded volumes.

Overview of the Element

The remainder of the Element proceeds to discuss, in brief, how religious nationalism has developed in India, Pakistan, and Sri Lanka. Section 1 provides a brief overview of the theoretical foundations of both nationalism and religious nationalism. Additionally, the section provides some essential background information to give the reader context before proceeding into the case studies. Section 2 explores the meteoritic rise of Sikh nationalism in the late twentieth century. Although Sikh nationalism had a well-established history, it quickly escalated during the Green Revolution in the 1970s and reached its height in the mid-1980s. It mostly subsided by the 1990s following years of counterinsurgency operations by India alongside the death, moderation, or migration of many Sikh militants.

Section 3 explores the dynamic development of Hindu nationalism in India over the past one hundred years. Hindu nationalism went from the margins of Indian society during the colonial era to fully engrained in the ruling BJP's policies by the twenty-first century. Several events have shaped the development of Hindu nationalism in India, most specifically the 1947 partition, the associated communal violence, and its lasting legacy of unsettled borders, specifically in Kashmir. The 1970s' Emergency under Indira Gandhi and her party's targeting of critics, particularly the Rashtriya Swayamsevak Sangh (RSS), helped empower the group and its ideology. The 1992 destruction of the Babri Masjid in Ayodhya, Uttar Pradesh, by Hindu nationalists served as a key milestone for the movement, representing a turning point by which Hindu nationalism had demonstrably merged into an increasingly powerful and mobilizing political ideology.

Section 4 traces the development of Islamic nationalism in Pakistan over time as the newly established country attempted to determine what role Islam would play in its identity and governance. Pakistan's early failure to establish a clear role for Islam within the state would haunt its legacy. Strong democratic institutions could never be effectively established, and this allowed the military to continue to erode civilian governance within the state. Over time, the military increased its power within the country and developed close ties with Islamic extremists to help target India within Kashmir and Soviets in Afghanistan. As Pakistan continued to experience political instability, the military's close ties with conservative Islamic elements increasingly shaped Pakistan's political identity. By the 1980s, under Zia-ul-Haq, Pakistan had increasingly Islamized its institutions and constitution specifically to define who is and is not a Muslim. Although Pakistan went through varying levels of democratic openness, the power of the military could not be suppressed. Despite Pakistan's alliance with the United States in the early twenty-first century in the global war on terror, Pakistan generally embraced Islamic nationalism as a policy. This was made even more clear under the administration of Imran Khan, who has praised the Taliban in Afghanistan and formally established state religious councils that increase Islamic education in public schools. The council also oversees whether blasphemy has been committed.

The final case study, in Section 5, explores the development and transformation of Buddhist nationalism within Sri Lanka. Nationalism in Sri Lanka began as a movement originally centered around language protection and later evolved to one that passed policies limiting citizenship and cultural rights of Tamils. These policies gave rise to the resistance movement led by the LTTE that escalated into a civil war that lasted from the 1970s until May 2009. Since then, the movement has evolved from one that primarily targeted Tamils to one that increasingly mobilizes against the Muslim minority. Buddhism and the Sinhala language took precedence since Sri Lanka's early independent formation and continue to hold the highest importance within the country. Despite initial democratic liberalization since the end of the civil war and promises of reconciliatory efforts, little progress has been made. Instead, communal violence and exclusionary measures by a government sympathetic to Buddhist nationalism predominate.

Section 6 concludes with an overview of all the cases explored in the Element. Section 6 helps the reader understand the key differences and similarities among the movements and how their continued trajectory may shape local, regional, and global politics. While South Asia and its experiences are unique, understanding how religious nationalism has manifested in the region provides a stronger and more nuanced understanding of a broader global phenomenon that is increasingly common.

1 Theoretical Approaches to Religious Nationalism

Nations and Nationalism

Religious nationalism cannot be understood without first examining the origins and concepts of nationalism, which has competing understandings and has been dynamic based on the historical period under examination. To discuss nationalism, it is first necessary to understand its various interpretations. In one of the most influential writings on nationalism, Benedict Anderson describes a nation as an "imagined political community that is both inherently limited and sovereign" (Anderson 2006: 7). According to Anderson, members of a nation will not know or interact with most of their fellow members. However, through the bond of the nation, a member will feel connected to other members.

One of the key thinkers in nationalism studies is Anthony Smith, who described nationalism as originally conceived as an "inclusive and liberating force" that helped overthrow "foreign imperial and colonial administrations" and generally promoted popular democracy (Smith 1998: 1). However, this rather optimistic view, whereby nationalism was seen as a modern source that could transcend ethnic and religious divisions, was relatively short-lived. Instead, ethnic and religious divisions have come to define many states both within the West and in postcolonial states. Smith continues his definition by claiming that national identity is defined by sameness through shared ancestry, language, territory, religion, history, and a general "feeling" of belonging to the group (Smith 1998: 1).

Scholars such as Hroch (1985) discuss the origins of nationalism and contend that it is an extension of cultural elites seeking to define themselves through a common history, and once established, that identity is used to politicize cross-class groups. Other scholars argue that attributes such as language and religion are used to define national identity into either an ethnic or civic dimension (Jones and Smith 2001; Björklund 2006). Other scholars such as Diez-Medrano (2005) argue that national identity is constructed based on exclusionary categories, in other words, who does not belong to the in-group. Gellner (2008), another well-known scholar of nationalism, contends that it emerges as states industrialize and strive for a singular culture within the modern state. This is often achieved through the adoption of things such as a national language and formal standardized education.

Nationalism and religious nationalism are not mutually exclusive. In fact, nationalism has historically been able to mobilize diverse groups despite differences in pursuit of a common goal, such as liberation from a colonizing force. It is more in the postcolonial era that nationalism has been increasingly tied to religious identity as a means of marginalizing and determining who does not belong within the state.

Religious Nationalism

Religion, as frequently analyzed in Western academia, is very much a product of colonial construction. Chatterjee (1993) discusses how religion, in the way the West understands it, was in many ways imposed categorically upon the population and based on perceived primordial categories. This was reinforced through colonial censuses that attempted to construct boundaries between beliefs and practices that were often more cross-cutting, such as Bhakti or Sufism (Shani 2020: 34). This allowed colonial administers to define religious and social categories more easily, particularly within South Asia, and ultimately to reinforce divisions (Kaviraj 2010). This led to what Georgio Shani (2020) terms the "thinning out of religious identities," eliminating unique historical and cultural spiritual practices to create more simply defined categories beneficial to colonial administers. For Hindus, it also allowed a particular type of Brahmin-centric Hinduism to broadly define the religion.

The censuses also came with problems that exacerbated existing group divisions and thus added to the anxiety of the dominant group regarding its population vis-à-vis other minorities. For example, in 1909, U. N. Mukherji wrote a pamphlet entitled "Hindus: A Dying Race" in which he warned Hindus of an impending demographic shift due to mass conversions of Hindus to Christianity and Islam (Mukherji 1909). In India and Pakistan, the traumatizing experience of the 1947 partition would greatly impact Hindus, Sikhs, and Muslims. The post-partition discourse was then one that changed the past perception of India as a multiethnic country into one that "territorialized nation-states" (Shani 2020). For Sri Lanka, the British and missionary practice of rapidly creating English schools and coincidently converting the population to Christianity in Tamil-dominated areas led to an increase in language nationalism that later merged into a linguistic-religious movement that sought to protect Sinhala and, by extension, Buddhism.

The fusing of religion and nationalism so that the two are indistinguishable is one way to understand religious nationalism (Rieffer 2003). Both nationalism and religion provide a sense of belonging and order for their adherents and both are tied to histories, iconographies, and myths that connect the community as a common unit with similar goals. The nation and religion provide guidelines on "behavior, belief, and belonging" (Wald and Wilcox 2006). When religion and nationalism fuse, the nation becomes defined by religion (Greenfeld 1996). Nationalism alone seeks political recognition and the sovereignty of a nation, and religion may or may not be a part of that identity.

Popular identification with religious nationalism is increasing, is often tied to ethnic identity, and has generally been electorally beneficial for political parties of the majority religion. The growing number of political parties running on a platform of religious nationalism has intensified the strength of previously weaker, more marginalized movements. At the core of modern religious nationalism is an opposition to some or all elements of the secular Westernized world. How this opposition manifests and what type of secularism the nationalists oppose varies. Religious nationalists may see decreased community participation in religious activities and events as a threat to long-term survival. Or it could be the absence, or increasing absence, of religion's influence on political affairs such as the lack of prayer in schools or the lack of displays of religious icons on government property. Religious nationalism generally rejects other religions' interpretations of moral codes, citizenship, history, and even economic outlooks (Grzymala-Busse 2019). Consequently, the movement often emphasizes a single religious identity while marginalizing religious minorities.

The role of religion in nationalism has been widely discussed with far-ranging interpretations. On one hand, scholars have argued that religion and nation act as substitutes, with religion providing its citizens with belonging before the nation-state existed (O'Brien 1994; Armstrong 1997; Hastings 1997). On the other hand, scholars argue that religious nationalism is a by-product of modernity making religion and national identities incompatible. In this instance, nationalism replaces religion or even becomes the religion (Hayes 1960; Tamir 1995). The modern nationalist view then begins to have overlapping elements of fascism, where the state has a singular identity and those that do not adhere to the identity do not belong to the state. This modernist view is largely a reflection of a Western interpretation of nationalism where religion is often compartmentalized into a separate identity. Such a compartmentalization of identities is less pronounced in much of Asia, specifically in South Asia, where religion and nation have increasingly bonded, leaving those who do not belong to the religion on the margins (Gorski and Türkmen-Dervişoğlu 2013; Grzymala-Busse 2019).

The literature on religious nationalism has straddled many disciplines. Scholars of religion, sociology, psychology, and political science have all used different theoretical groundings to understand the evolution, motivations, and goals of religious nationalist movements and the individuals who join them. South Asia nationalism scholar Peter van de Veer describes religious nationalism as a form of nationalism built on existing religious communities with a concern for demonstrating the historical existence of their nation (Van de Veer 1994). He also describes nationalist movements in South Asia as dependent, meaning they influence and grow from one another, so when Hindu nationalism thrives, Muslim nationalism grows and vice versa. This can clearly be seen with the cases of India and Pakistan, as Sections 3 and 4 demonstrate.

One of the leading scholars on religious nationalism, Mark Juergensmeyer (1996), classifies religious nationalism into three categories: ethnic, ideological, and ethno-ideological. Ethnic religious nationalism ties the people and their history, including their religion, to the land. In this type of nationalism, there are generally two broad groups, an oppressor and the oppressed. Nationalists typically see themselves as oppressed and their identities at risk due to the oppressor. Ethnic religious nationalism has been especially dominant in South Asia. Other movements such as the separatist movements of Kashmiri Muslims and Irish Catholics also fell along ethnic lines. This type of nationalism has escalated into genocide in certain cases, specifically the case of the former Yugoslavia and the Orthodox Serbs, Catholic Croats, and Muslim Bosnians.

The ideological form of religious nationalism works in the opposite direction by putting political struggles into a religious context. This has been especially common with many Islamic movements such as the Iranian revolution. Juergensmeyer (1996) notes that while the enemy of the ethnic nationalists is another ethnic group, for ideological religious groups, the enemy is often within their own ethnic group. Secular political leaders are one such example, as has been demonstrated in Pakistan when more progressive leaders like Zulfiqar Ali Bhutto are in power. For many Islamic groups, anyone who opposes their specific theological vision is seen as an enemy. The Muslim Brotherhood, al-Qaeda, and ISIS all saw secular political leaders as the enemy because of their alignment with secular and Western principles. In Israel, a Jewish nationalist killed Yitzhak Rabin for his cooperation with Palestinians who were working toward a two-state solution.

Ethno-ideological religious nationalism combines these two characteristics. In such instances, the enemy falls along both ethnic and ideological lines. For example, in Palestine, Hamas challenged not only the Israelis but also secular leaders such as Yasir Arafat. The Sikh separatists also had ethnic and ideological motivations. Sikh nationalists and their goal of an independent Sikh Khalistan state are mostly tied to Punjabi ethnicity and the state of Punjab. Khalistan supporters attempted to remove Hindus throughout Punjab in order to create a Sikh state. The Buddhist nationalist movement in Sri Lanka is strongly tied to Sinhalese ethnicity, yet also considers Sinhalese secular leaders as a concurrent enemy.

Juergensmeyer (1996) contends that religious nationalism arises from the failures of secular nationalism. Emerging fundamental movements, especially in former colonies, may seek to reject Western and secular ideas of how a nation is constructed and operated. Instead, the movements may seek a return to the precolonial era before colonization and Western ideas corrupted the population and its religion. Given these distinct and often overlapping categories of nationalism, how do the goals of groups vary and what are the underlying grievances? In all the cases examined in this Element, there is a general theme of rejecting "Western" ideas such as diversity, secularism, and pluralism.

In India and Sri Lanka, as Sections 3 and 5 discuss, religious nationalists seek to return to the era before colonization. Buddhist nationalists long for the days before British colonization when Buddhist kingdoms were dominant. Hindu nationalists seek to return to the pre-Mughal era, a time they consider the beginning of Hindu marginalization. Not surprisingly, this has led scholars to consider nationalism in both Sri Lanka and India as fused with religious myths and symbolism (Friedland 2001). Thus, it is not surprising that religious architecture and similar symbolisms have been at the forefront of movements in both countries. In Pakistan, as Section 4 discusses, many radical Muslim schools of thought seek to promote a pure vision of Islam like the one seen during the time of the prophet Muhammad in the seventh century.

The explanations for what give rise to religious nationalism vary. Friedland (2001) suggests that the more removed the state is from matters of religion, such as India and the United States, the higher the likelihood of religious nationalism. For one, such a view allows religious groups to explore and challenge existing religious hierarchies. Because religious nationalism is creating competition in the marketplace of religious ideas, each establishment seeking to win more adherents may resort to more extreme ideas to help win over the population.

Religious diversity can help create religious nationalism as the dominant group sees such diversity as a threat to its demographic dominance (Bloom, Arikan, and Courtemanche 2015). Consequently, as is seen in India and Sri Lanka, diversity can lead to exclusionary ideas and policies. This is not surprising since a frequent companion of nationalism is xenophobia and fear of the constructed "outsider." This exclusion creates tension among the groups and can lead to a rise in violence by the nationalists and by their targets (Juergensmeyer 2003). For example, references to acts of violence against Muslims throughout India have been used as a recruitment method by Islamist groups throughout India and the world (Vicziany 2007).

When the majority in-group perceives a threat from a minority out-group, it can result in acts of prejudice that escalate into violence and stronger national identification (Stephan and Stephan 1996; Bizman and Yinon 2001; Esses et al. 2001). This dynamic is evident throughout India as demonstrated by its long history of riots and intercommunal tensions between Hindus and other religious minorities, especially Muslims (Van de Veer 1994; Tausch, Hewstone, and Roy 2009). Likewise, as nationalist sentiment increased in Pakistan, so too did sectarian violence, particularly targeting Shias, Sufis, and Ahmadis. In Sri Lanka, excessive national identification escalated into a civil war for nearly thirty years. Even when the war ended, the nationalist forces within the country regrouped with increased communal targeting of the Muslim population. The violence in all countries confirms the findings of many authors. When the majority in-group perceives the minority group as threatening their values and ways of life, they will respond with increased hostility (Lahav 2004; Sniderman, Hagendoorn, and Prior 2004).

Backgrounds on Religious Nationalism in India, Pakistan, and Sri Lanka

In India, the political consolidation of the Hindu nationalist paramilitary organization, the RSS, with the ruling BJP means Hindu nationalism has become the primary platform of a party that relies almost entirely on Hindu voting blocs. Hindu nationalism operates under the assumption that although Hindus are a large majority within their country, their majority status is under increasing threat. According to Hindu nationalists, this threat emanates primarily from Muslim expansionism via illegal immigration from bordering Muslim countries, high birth rates, and forced religious conversion of Hindu women coerced into marriage with Muslim men, a practice referred to as "love jihad." Hindu nationalists also voice concerns about evangelical Christianity. Evangelical Christians are accused of providing economic incentives to low-caste Hindus as a means of escaping the caste system. Derogatory phrases such as "rice bag convert" are frequently used to describe those who convert to Christianity in hopes of a return of material goods like rice (Dhoss 2014).

Religious nationalism in independent India has not only been dominated by Hindus. Prior to the increased prominence of Hindu nationalism, Sikh nationalists led a violent campaign to establish Khalistan, an independent homeland for Sikhs in Punjab. The Sikh militancy movement is perhaps most well known for its escalation that ultimately led to the death of Prime Minister Indira Gandhi. Prime Minister Gandhi's assassination at the hands of her Sikh bodyguards was considered revenge for her leadership during Operation Blue Star (OBS), a military operation that stormed Sikhism's holiest site, the Golden Temple. Operation Blue Star resulted in the deaths of hundreds of Sikh pilgrims and key militant leadership. Additionally, the architectural damage inflicted upon a Sikh sacred space was a visual reminder of state-led violence. Unlike the current Hindu nationalist movement led by the adherents of a majority religion, Sikh nationalism arose in response to a perceived economic inequality that was met with brute state violence and oppression.

Since its birth in 1947, Pakistan cannot be separated from its complicated divisions among language, culture, religion, and geography. Pakistan was founded as a refuge for South Asian Muslims. The role of Islam was never clearly elucidated at Pakistan's founding and led to much internal contention about the extent of Islam's role in the state's governance and identity. Since then, Pakistan has been plagued by internal instability, weak democratic institutions, and growing Islamic extremism. A clear hierarchy emerged from independence onward that situated Urdu-speaking Punjabis at the top of the hierarchy and non-Urdu-speaking non-Punjabis at the lower end. This led to multiple fractures within Pakistan that escalated into violent campaigns from East Pakistan (modern Bangladesh) to Baluchistan along the Afghanistan border. Existing discontent in East Pakistan escalated once the Bengali-led Awami League won national elections but was not seated by the ruling West Pakistan establishment. Bengali resistance was met with a harsh crackdown, known as Operation Spotlight, by the West Pakistan government. West Pakistan coalesced with Islamists in Bangladesh to commit systematic acts of violence that many consider genocide (Beachler 2007). The war led to millions of refugees and the involvement of India. East Pakistan eventually achieved its independence and became Bangladesh. The events of 1971 as well as the ongoing conflicts with India over Kashmir have undoubtedly shaped the nationalistic version of Islam seen in modern Pakistan. The significant influence of the military over supposedly civilian institutions has also defined Pakistan's version of religious nationalism. The military has continued to provide varying levels of support for Islamist extremist groups, particularly those that operate in Kashmir and Afghanistan, in order to advance its regional geopolitical goals.

In addition to the conflicts with India and Bangladesh, Pakistan also increasingly marginalized its religious minorities, especially the Ahmadiyya. When the founding father of Pakistan, Muhammad Ali Jinnah, was asked about the religious status of the Ahmadiyya, he replied, "Who am I to declare a person non-Muslim who calls himself a Muslim?" However, Jinnah's death within one year of independence meant much of his vision, including his feelings toward the Ahmadiyya, was not followed by future leadership. By 1974, the second amendment was added to the Pakistan constitution under Bhutto, declaring who is non-Muslim, with specific reference to Ahmadis. "'Non-Muslim' means a person who is not a Muslim and includes a person belonging to the Christian, Hindu, Sikh, Buddhist or Parsi community, a person of the Quadiani Group or the Lahori Group who call themselves 'Ahmadis' or by any other name or a Bahai, and a person belonging to any of the Scheduled Castes" (Constitution of Pakistan, Article 260, clause C).

By 1984, President Zia-ul-Haq, who came to power via a coup, continued targeting the Ahmadi by passing an ordinance that Ahmadis cannot call themselves Muslim or "pose as Muslims" or else they will face three years in prison. Since then, the Ahmadiyya have faced increasing levels of persecution. Religious minorities including Shia, Sufi, and Christians have also been vulnerable to multiple attacks by Islamists amid a government that has varied in its commitment to reducing Islamic extremism within its borders. All these factors combined shape the complicated dynamics of Islamic nationalism in modern Pakistan, which has been multifaceted and played varying roles depending upon the political leadership.

Buddhist nationalism has also become increasingly prevalent in the twenty-first century and has close ties to the current ruling party in Sri Lanka. In Sri Lanka, Buddhist nationalism has been explicitly tied to Sinhalese ethnicity and language. However, with time, the linguistic and ethnic nationalist elements have decreased since the Sinhala language has been well integrated into the state and the Sinhalese people hold the majority of power. In exchange, Buddhism has become increasingly emphasized over language. Because Sri Lanka is seen as the only homeland for Sinhalese Buddhists, paramilitary Buddhist groups led by monks seek to protect the Buddhist identity of Sri Lanka. Like Hindu nationalism,

Buddhist nationalism asserts an existential threat from religious minorities, specifically Muslims and Hindu Tamils. In Sri Lanka, Buddhist nationalists utilize tactics including economic boycotts of Muslims, bans on Islamic clothing, accusations of Buddhist sterilization by Muslims, and riots targeting Muslim homes and businesses. The state has also continued to target Tamil critics and journalists with forced disappearances, destruction of war memorials, and the pardoning of accused war criminals (Mittal 2021).

Sri Lanka has a long history of denying citizenship rights to the minority Tamil Hindus. The Ceylon Citizenship Act (1948) effectively stripped the citizenship of Tamils who came to Sri Lanka during colonial rule and set the tone for the future goals of the state, one where Buddhism is given "the foremost place" and whereby the state has a duty to "protect and foster the Buddha Sasana." Buddhist nationalism in Sri Lanka increased in power and scope during the thirty-year civil war with the LTTE. Following the end of the civil war, Buddhist nationalists focused their discontent on Muslims, leading to increased violence targeting Muslims. The 2015 election of Maithripala Sirisena appeared to promise a new age of ethnic reconciliation, but within a few years the hope quickly faded amid the 2018 constitutional crisis and the 2019 Easter attacks by the Islamic extremist group National Thowheeth Jama'ath, which killed 269. Following the 2019 Easter attacks in Sri Lanka, former defense minister Gotabaya Rajapaksa announced his candidacy for president. Rajapaksa ran on a platform with the goal of dismantling Islamic extremism. Rajapaksa, who was the defense minister at the height of the Sri Lankan civil war and was accused of war crimes, was viewed favorably by much of the Sinhalese electorate for his historic ability to counter violent movements by any means necessary. He remained closely aligned with the Buddhist nationalist monks within the country and centered their ideas within his campaign. In August 2020, Rajapaksa's brother and the former president, Mahinda, ran on a similar platform and was elected as prime minister.

Sikh nationalism demonstrates that nationalist movements can end and transition into traditional political engagement. However, the likelihood of defeat is greater when the nationalist movement is led by a minority religion with limited access to power structures. In contrast, nationalist movements led by majority religions with close ties to political parties, such as

Hinduism in India, Islam in Pakistan, and Buddhism in Sri Lanka, face fewer constraints. In such cases, the ruling parties use their power to limit the rights of religious minorities.

The cases explored here can help readers understand nationalism in a more general manner while also demonstrating the uniqueness of religious nationalism in South Asia. When a nationalist movement is led by a minority, like the Sikhs in India, its goals will likely be autonomy or independence. When members of the majority lead a nationalist movement, like Hindus in India, Buddhists in Sri Lanka, and Muslims in Pakistan, they will use their power to limit the agency of the minority through tactics such as limiting movement, expressions of identity, education, or citizenship. In all cases, the threat to democracy is strong and the likelihood of violence is high.

2 Sikh Nationalism

Sikh nationalism is the only case explored in this Element that is primarily a movement of the past, at least at the time of writing. Including this case study gives the advantage of hindsight, which can then be used to understand current and future cases. Sikh nationalism is also the only example here that explores the rise of nationalism in a religious minority group (see Figure 2). The remaining cases are nationalists who come from the majority religious group of their respective countries. This key difference may also help explain the difference in the goals and strategies of Sikhs compared to those of Hindus and Buddhists. Separatism was the strategy of Sikhs because they felt their identity was being threatened by a state that was unwilling to compromise. The willingness of the state to utilize escalating violence, particularly on Sikh holy sites, increased discontent and radicalized even previously apolitical Sikhs. Moreover, many Sikhs felt independence would help correct historical wrongs committed at their expense.

Key Beliefs of Sikh Nationalists

At its height, Sikh nationalism was among the most organized separatist movements in the world. While elements of Sikh nationalism survive in the twenty-first century, the core of the movement and its secessionist goals

India Religious Demographics

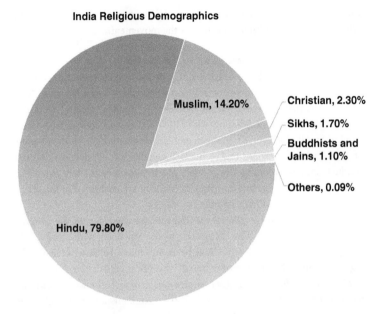

Figure 2 India Religious Demographics

have been placated. Sikh nationalists sought to establish autonomy at a minimum and an expansive independent state with aspirations as far as New Delhi at a maximum. Literature on the topic has attempted to explain the origins and trajectory of the movement and has identified several key factors. The most popular explanation in literature is that Sikh nationalism was primarily a response to increasingly violent and authoritarian actions by Indira Gandhi's administration (Gellner 2008). Critical scholars emphasize the role of socioeconomic inequality and the strategies of elite Jat farmers in Punjab to control rural workers (Gill and Singhal 1984; Purewal 2012). Other authors have explored the impact of the well-organized Sikh diaspora (Tatla 2005). Authors like Shani, however, recognize the overlapping impact of all these features on the Sikh nationalist movement (2008). The following sections explore the historical background and rise of Sikh nationalism and the ultimate decline of the movement.

Emergence of the Khalsa

Sikhism emerged in the fifteenth century in the Punjab region of modern India. Sikhism is a monotheistic religion founded by Guru Nanak (1469–1539). Sikhs (*sikh* meaning learner or seeker in Punjabi) follow the teachings of the ten gurus beginning with Guru Nanak and ending with Guru Govind Singh (1666–1708). Sikhism emphasizes meditation on the oneness of God, selfless service, unity, justice, equality of all humans, honest conduct, and overcoming lust, rage, greed, attachment, and ego. The foundational teachings and concepts of Sikhism are enshrined in the scripture known as Guru Granth Sahib.

The birth and major growth of Sikhism occurred during the Mughal empire (1526–1857). The Mughals were Muslims with origins in Turkestan. Although Muslims had been present in India as early as the eighth century, the first major sultanate was not established in New Delhi until 1206. By 1526, the Mughal empire was established under Babur and its territory stretched from modern-day Afghanistan to Bangladesh. Babur's expansionist grandson, Akbar the Great, arrived in Punjab and viewed Sikhs favorably, even donating land to them (Atwal 2021). However, after Akbar's death in 1605, the tensions between the Mughals and Sikhs intensified. Akbar's successor, Jahangir, ascended to the throne and took a contentious approach to the Sikhs (Shoeb, Warriach, and Chawla 2015). According to Sikh tradition, Jahangir asked Guru Arjun Dev (1563–1606) to convert to Islam and to change passages in the Guru Granth Sahib so they would speak of Islam more favorably (Singh 2014). Jahangir already disliked Arjun Dev for supporting the rebellion of Khusrau Mirza, Jahnagir's son. When the guru refused to convert or change scripture, he was tortured for five days, leading to his death. Guru Arjan's son, Guru Hargobind (1595–1645), the sixth guru, saw his father's death as an act of martyrdom, and Arjun Dev is generally viewed as the first Sikh martyr (Singh 2014). Guru Arjan's death transformed Sikhism's approach to defending the faith (Fenech 2001). Guru Hargobind established a Sikh army and saw the Sikhs as a sovereign people (Mahmood 1996).

In 1628, Shah Jahan, the emperor at the time, assaulted the Sikhs' holy center of Amritsar and pushed the Sikhs into retreat in Kashmir. Guru Hargobind then died in 1645, tortured to death like his predecessor. The ninth guru, Guru Tegh Bahudur (1621–1675), made pilgrimages into Kashmir in defiance of Mughal leader Aurangzeb to aid Hindu Kashmiri Pandits who sought to avoid conversion to Islam. When the Mughals captured Bahudur, they gave him the option to convert or die. He chose death (Seiple 2013). Bahudur's son, Govind Singh (1666–1708), the tenth and final guru, incensed by the persecution of his predecessors, transformed the Sikh identity into one of sacred defense of the faith (Dhavan 2011).

Sikhism was founded upon historical persecution that significantly impacted the trajectory of the Sikh identity. With this transformation came the establishment of a community of warriors known as the Khalsa. The Khalsa abided by a faith-based dress code that reflected the Sikh soldier of faith. Elements of this dress code included carrying a sword known as the *kirpan* along with other identifiers like a metal bracelet known as the *kara* and not cutting hair. The *kirpan* was both a symbol of the Sikh obligation to defend the faith and a practical tool intended for defense. Govind sought to make Sikhs easily identifiable to those within and outside the community. Alongside this identity was the establishment of the Khalsa army. While the Khalsa army was an important historical development, it was not universal. The Nanakpanthis, for example, continued to practice the mysticism and nonviolent approach associated with Guru Nanak (Mahmood 1989).

Guru Singh and his newly established Khalsa army sought to overthrow the Mughal state in order to avenge the death of his predecessors. Although he was not successful, the legacy of his religious transformation of Sikh identity and expression continued. No longer were the Sikh leaders acting to defend their faith. They were willing to seek retaliation for previous wrongdoings. Singh clarified that defense of the faith is the only acceptable use of force and that force should be used only

after all other alternatives have been attempted (Mahmood 1989).
Nevertheless, he declared:

> The army of the Guru will sit on the throne of Delhi
> Over its head will be carried the umbrella of royalty, and its will
>   shall be done
> The Khalsa will rule, their enemies will be vanquished,
> Only those that seek refuge will be saved. (Platteau 2017: 333)

This quote demonstrates the willingness of the movement to use violence to
achieve its goals and challenge its enemies. The mention of Delhi displays
a willingness to expand far beyond the goal of autonomy within Punjab.
This poem would prove foundational for the Sikh separatist movement in
the 1980s.

When the Mughal empire began its decline, the *misl*s, or individual
territories, were united into a singular Sikh state known as the Sikh Raj or
Sarkar-a-Khalsa. Maharaja Ranjit Singh (1780–1839) led the unified state
and is considered the father of the Sikh empire. Despite being Sikh,
Maharaja Singh operated under secular standards and included Hindus
and Muslims in his operations (Roy 2011). As king, he oversaw the construction of Sikhism's most holy site, the Harmandir Sahib. During his rule,
he defeated multiple invasions from Afghanistan, Persia, and broader
Central Asia and expanded the territory beyond modern Punjab to parts
of modern Pakistan and much of Kashmir (Lafont 2002). He also maintained diplomatic relations with the British and even signed agreements
with them recognizing the territory of the Sikh empire (Atwal 2021). The
friendliness was short-lived, however.

The Sikh empire declined rapidly after Ranjit Singh died in 1839.
Following Ranjit Singh's death came internal clashes for power and
rising anti-British sentiment that ultimately resulted in the Sikh army
attacking the British in 1845, starting the first British–Sikh war (Smith
2019). The Sikhs utilized the ideology of Khalsa and the defense of the
faith to drive their offensive response to the British. The Sikhs were
defeated within three months and the British took control of the
territory. The Sikhs again fought a war with the British from 1848

to 1849, a war that eliminated the Sikh government and resulted in direct rule of the territory by the British. The British, impressed by the Sikhs' tactical abilities and their loyalty to the British during the Indian rebellion of 1857–1858, recruited Sikhs for the British–Indian army (Khalidi 2001). The Sikhs would become an important component of the British–Indian army, fighting in major battles against invading Afghan forces, the Opium Wars in China, World War I, and World War II (Thampi 1999). Sikh faith became fused with a warrior identity. Sikh soldiers on the front lines were often seen carrying the Guru Granth Sahib and their *kirpan* in addition to modern artillery.

The Sikhs' loyalty to the British began to wane by the end of World War I amid the growth of nationalist independence movements throughout the country. British concern of insurrections by the Sikhs led to violent clampdowns, including the Jallianwala Bagh Massacre in 1919, when the British army fired on a peaceful group of civilians gathering in the religious square during a curfew (Raghaven 2005). The massacre likely killed a thousand civilians and was a key event not only for Sikhs but for all of India to push for independence.

The emergence of Sikhism at a time of transformational change in India undoubtedly impacted Sikh views and the trajectory of Sikhs' utilization of violence. Sikhs' training in the British–Indian army allowed them to develop expertise in modern weaponry. The death and persecution of the gurus by the Mughals and the later British subjugation created a sense of necessity to defend the faith. Sikhism became associated with warriorhood, and that identity would remain an important part of how Sikhs perceived themselves once India gained independence in 1947.

Rise of Sikh Nationalism

When India was partitioned in 1947, Punjab found itself at the center of the conflict. Bengal and Punjab were two Muslim-majority provinces that eventually split during the partition. As the new boundaries were determined, Sikhs were essentially excluded from the conversation (Chandra 2016). The partition lines were hastily drawn by Sir Cyril Radcliffe, a British civil servant with little regard for the history and dynamics of the region. The partition ultimately escalated into unprecedented levels of violence and mass human movement. Punjab became the epicenter of violence because it was a key path for Hindus and Sikhs coming to India and for Muslims going to Pakistan. Along the way, clashes broke out that devastated Sikh villages. The newly independent government and the departing British government were not prepared to intervene, and the violence escalated. Exact estimates are difficult, but two hundred thousand to 2 million people died during the partition and more than 10 million were displaced (Talbot and Singh 2009: 2). By the end, Muslims had a homeland in Pakistan, and Hindus were the majority in a secular India, but many Sikhs remained excluded. This feeling of exclusion would continue to grow in the following decades.

As the independence movement in India grew, Jawaharlal Nehru (1889–1964), considered the founder of independent India, attempted to satiate Sikh leaders by promising they would experience the "glow of freedom" if they joined Nehru's cause and stayed in India (Dhillon 1974). The specifics of this seemingly vague promise to Sikhs were unclear. Many Sikh leaders interpreted "freedom" as giving a homeland to Sikhs within India (Shani 2008). However, in Nehru's commitment to secularism, he wanted to avoid organizing state boundaries based on religion (Jalal 1998). India's constitution adopted a general commitment to secularism. However, the Indian concept of secularism did not prevent varying levels of state-led interference in religious affairs. Such interference was seen as problematic by Sikhs, who were also upset at their classification as Hindu under the broad religious umbrella (Mahmood 1989).

As early as 1940, Sikh intellectuals such as Dr. V. S. Bhatti began promoting the idea of Khalistan, an independent Sikh state (Bianchini et al. 2004). As Muslims put forth their desire for greater autonomy, Sikhs made similar demands. Many Sikhs worried their religion could not survive without an independent state (Shani 2008). Sikh leaders began advocating for varying solutions they hoped would remedy their concerns, such as separating Muslim-majority districts from Sikh-majority districts and guaranteeing representation for Sikhs in the Punjab legislature (Shani 2008). Sikh organizations such as the Shiromani Akali Dal (SAD) advocated for Sikh representation and empowerment in independent India. When it became increasingly clear to Sikhs that the state would do little to give their community ensured recognition and representation, Sikh calls for independence grew. Given the majoritarian structure of the government, Sikhs knew they couldn't gain veritable representation on the national political scene. From 1956 to 1964, Sikh leaders, including SAD and Punjab's chief minister, adopted the strategy of infiltrating the dominant Indian National Congress (INC) party in order to exert pressure (Shani 2008). However, within that eight-year period, Sikh leaders felt minimal progress had been made (Singh 2000: 107).

The failure of the INC's infiltration tactic led to a change in strategy and to the adoption of *morchas*, nonviolent agitation by Akali Dal. Sikhs had historically utilized *morchas* during colonial-era confrontations with the British (Grewal 1998). *Morchas* usually started as rallies rich in religious symbolism within the *gurudwara*, or place of worship, and moved outside, seeking arrest through agitation (1955–1961). The strategy ultimately resulted in the arrest of thousands of Sikh demonstrators but made minimal progress toward the goal of autonomy or independence (Shani 2008).

Because religious-based states contradicted the idea of a secular India, Sikhs shifted their strategy of statehood to focus on language in their Punjabi Suba strategy (Kohli 1997). Sikh activists sought a Punjabi language–based state, a strategy Indira Gandhi eventually accepted in 1966 with the Punjab Reorganisation Act (Grewal 1998). The new act divided Punjabi-speaking Punjab into a new state and carved Haryana out as a Hindi-speaking state. To the discontent of many Sikhs, Chandigarh was also removed from Punjab and made into a union territory (Grewal 1998). With this change, Sikhs became the majority in Punjab. This new state, however, was not sufficient for many Sikhs who still longed for an independent Khalistan.

Akali Dal at its core always had nationalist goals, including independence, with autonomy as a first step (Shani 2008). Oberoi (1987) discussed how territoriality became a defining feature of Sikh identity. Despite achieving what nominally constituted a Sikh state, forthcoming measures in Punjab, like the Green Revolution, accelerated the turn to Sikh militancy. Punjab is often referred to as the breadbasket of India because of the fertile nature of its soil. The Green Revolution began in 1965 as part of a Congress-led initiative to modernize India's food production. The revolution was intended to transition to farming methods that created a greater wheat yield and lowered dependency on outside countries for food. By 1970, Punjab was producing 70 percent of all food grains in India (Sandhu 2014). Punjabis had traditionally been employed in agriculture, so the Green Revolution impacted them perhaps more than any other group. While the revolution did indeed increase crop output and promote economic development, critics argued that it did so unevenly (Dhanagare 1988).

The revolution primarily aided the higher-caste Jat farmers while also creating a new class of landless laborers (Corsi 2006). Over the next decade, the overall wealth of Punjab flourished but so did inequality, absolute poverty, and unemployment (Dhanagare 1988). The central government also installed canals over local Punjab rivers that diverted local water to neighboring states to aid agricultural productivity (Betigeri 2014). These decisions by the central government created fractures within the community that began widening and contributed to increased anti-India sentiments.

In 1973, Akali Dal put forth the Anandpur Sahib Resolution, which sought increased autonomy from the central government for Punjab and recognition of Sikhism as a religion distinct from Hinduism (Singh 2004). The document mostly went unnoticed aside from the key members within the movement until Jarnail Singh Bhindranwale changed that trajectory. Bhindranwale was a militant Sikh and rising leader of the Khalistan movement. He sought an independent Sikh state and publicly opposed anyone, Sikh or not, who disagreed with him. Specifically, Bhindranwale focused his discontent on the Sant Nirankaris, a movement within Sikhism that originated in the nineteenth century and believed in a living guru (Juergensmeyer 1988). A 1978 clash between militant Sikhs and Sant Nirankaris killed sixteen people. This clash is considered the beginning of the escalation of violence in Punjab that ultimately started the insurgency (Tully and Jacob 2006).

As Bhindranwale's group, Damdani Taksal, increased its influence in the late 1970s, the INC saw Bhindranwale as a potential ally to counter Akali Dal, the INC's primary electoral opponent in Punjab (Bal 2019). The INC helped release Bhindranwale and his followers from prison and cleared them of murder charges stemming from their role in the death of Nirankaris (Bal 2019). Further, Congress supported him and his followers in the 1979 local elections in return for their support in the 1980 Punjab elections. This partnership would quickly unravel as Bhindranwale became more militant and aided in the assassination of Hindu Congress leader Lala Jagat Narain in 1981 (Singh 2000).

In August 1982, Bhindranwale declared the Dharam Yudh Morcha, essentially a religiously justified war in order to defend the Sikh faith and gain independence (Chima 1997). Yet the Dharam Yudh Morcha not only targeted the state or non-Sikhs. It also targeted Sikhs who did not share Bhindranwale's perspective. Bhindranwale asserted that the *morchas* would continue until all demands set forth in the Anandpur Sahib Resolution were met, specifically an autonomous or independent Khalistan (Shiromani Akali Dal 1973). At the same time, the SAD was actively working with Bhindranwale, boosting his influence. Over the next several months, acts of violence increased, which included more targeted assassinations (Shani 2008). Violent acts were occurring alongside the original acts of *morcha*, which led to the eventual arrests of twenty-five thousand *morcha* participants (Chima 2008). As militant Sikh leaders sought to disrupt the 1982 Asian Games in New Delhi with protests, INC leaders closed Punjab's border and instituted heavy searches of any Sikh who sought to attend (*New York Times* 1982). This act escalated anger toward the INC and served as a recruitment tool for the organization, including among retired Indian military servicemen like Major General Shabeg Singh, who became Bhindranwale's military advisor (Chima 1997).

Acts of violence drastically escalated in Punjab after 1982. Bhindranwale received an invitation from the militant youth wing of Akali Dal to move to the Golden Temple so as to prevent his arrest (Singh 2004). Bhindranwale moved into the temple in August 1982 and began stockpiling weapons. The Golden Temple was seen as a safe refuge: not only was it taboo for the government to attack religious sites, but an attack on the holiest place in Sikhism would have isolated even pro-India Sikhs. As attacks increased, Prime Minister Indira Gandhi suspended the state government and declared President's Rule on October 10, 1983, following the murder of six Hindu passengers on a bus. From the beginning of the declaration of Dharam Yudh Morcha until the launch of OBS in early June 1984, twelve hundred violent incidents took place at the hands of Sikh militants.

Amid the increasing militancy, diaspora groups, especially in Canada, began supporting the movement. Organizations such as Babar Khalsa, Khalistan Council, Dal Khalsa, World Sikh Organization, and International Sikh Youth Federation provided ample monetary support (Razavy 2006). On June 1, 1984, the Indian military entered the Golden Temple during OBS after numerous requests for Bhindranwale and his supporters to leave failed. Indian forces met extensive resistance from various members of the militant movement, including those armed with grenades and rifles. Although the Indian military had orders to not target the temple, the Akal Takht, a holy relic, received extensive damage. Estimates vary widely, but the official civilian death toll, according to the Indian government, was 492. The Indian government said most of the deaths, which included Bhindranwale, were militants, not civilians, although this is heavily disputed. The Indian military ended the operation with 83 dead and 249 injured. Sikh anger escalated to unprecedented levels.

In Canada, outraged Sikh leaders in the diaspora began speaking out. Ajaib Singh Bagri traveled throughout the country, promoting violence against India and Hindus (Fair 2006). Bagri is quoted as saying, " Until we kill 50,000 Hindus, we will not rest . . . The Indian Government is our enemy, the same way the Hindu society is our enemy . . . We are to die in the battlefield, fighting, by sacrificing ourselves. To die such a death, which is the mission of the Khalsa, is our religion" (Fair 2006).

Six months after OBS, on October 31, 1984, Indira Gandhi was assassinated by her Sikh bodyguards for her role in the operation. In response to Gandhi's assassination, wide-scale anti-Sikh violence erupted throughout the country, with allegations that INC members had provided the addresses of Sikhs' homes and businesses to the public (Pillalamari 2014). The immediate impact was riots and pogroms targeting Sikhs, estimated to have caused eight thousand to seventeen thousand deaths throughout forty cities (Pillalamari 2014). The militancy did not end with Prime Minister Gandhi's assassination. Instead, acts of violence escalated in the following years. New leaders emerged within the movement, in both Punjab and the diaspora. On June 23, 1985, Air India Flight 182 from

Toronto was bombed by a Canada-based Sikh nationalist group, Babbar Khalsa. Three hundred and twenty-nine people were killed. The incident was the worst aviation act of terrorism until 9/11.

Over the next decade, the militancy movement continued, which resulted in the estimated deaths of at least 12,000 civilians, 8,000 militants, and 1,417 members of the security forces (Central Intelligence Agency 2000). Despite Bhindranwale's death, his ideas and tactics remained. The goal of an independent Sikh state in the form of Khalistan stayed central. Sikh nationalists also contested and won elections in Punjab (Singh 2000). Under the leadership of the INC, the military continued to fight against a well-organized, militant Sikh movement. Alongside the widespread migration and death of militants, the movement began to lose power. The INC's political dominance also began to fracture after the assassination of Rajiv Gandhi (son of Indira) in 1991 by the LTTE. Sikh nationalists began to see alternative paths forward, including through political processes. In the face of losing power, the INC also sought to rectify relations with Sikh political leaders and return them to the party in the face of rising Hindu nationalism and growing regional parties (Kang 2005). Although its members were increasingly less diverse, the INC sought to present itself as an inclusive party. The INC made public initiatives to reintegrate Sikhs into the party such as when the INC embraced a regionalist discourse under Captain Amarinder Singh, a Sikh who had resigned from the INC after OBS (Shani 2008). Singh later became the chief minister of Punjab and helped abrogate the 1981 River Waters Treaty with neighboring states, addressing a key Akali grievance against the state. Sonia Gandhi, Rajiv Gandhi's widow and the new leader of the INC, also sought to incorporate Sikhs into the party and to focus on the issues of Punjab. By 1996, Manmohan Singh became a leader within the party. He became the first Sikh prime minister of India in 2004. This inclusion of Sikhs helped draw many Sikhs, formerly sympathetic to the militant cause, away from supporting the idea of Khalistan and to focus on Punjab. By the late 1990s, the movement had essentially diminished beyond elements of individual extremism within the community.

The Sikh nationalist movement serves as an excellent case study of the fluidity of a nationalist movement. Although Sikh group consciousness existed from the onset, outside events and persecution helped radically transform the trajectory of the religion and its followers. Sikhs began seeing the necessity to protect themselves and to identify as unique from neighboring Hindus and Muslims. Historical persecution by the Mughals led to the deaths of gurus. Later persecution by the British led to the loss of the Sikh state. The secular INC attempted to strip Sikhs of their identity and agency while manipulating them in order to advance the cause of the party. In sum, the short history of Sikhism was one of suffering and persecution. Sikhs saw the martyrdom of the gurus and ongoing persecution as the push needed to transform from a faith focused on nonviolence to one focused on defense.

In the remaining cases examined in Sections 3 through 5, the nationalists come from the majority religion in the country. Not only are the nationalists numerically more powerful, they are aided by their proximity to and representation within the government. Consequently, the approach of the Hindus, Muslims, and Buddhists is not one of separatism against the state, like the Sikhs. Instead, the Hindus, Muslims, and Buddhists utilize the state apparatus to restrict religious minorities through coerced assimilation and reduction of religious liberties and expression.

3 Hindu Nationalism in India

In March 2020, Tablighi Jamaat, a conservative Sunni Muslim missionary group, became a household name throughout India. COVID was on the verge of being declared a global pandemic, and some of India's first cases were tied to a Tablighi Jamaat gathering in New Delhi (Israelsen and Malji 2021). Local media and some BJP government officials accused the group members of holding a super-spreader event, calling them terrorists "moving around like a bomb" and thwarting lockdown rules, even though their meeting took place at least a week prior to the national lockdown (Press Trust of India 2020). The inciting language used toward Tablighi Jamaat is part of a larger Islamophobic narrative that has dominated much of the political rhetoric, social media, and cable news programming throughout India. Tablighi Jamaat received intense focus for several weeks and was blamed for the worsening COVID situation in India. In August 2020, a bench of the Bombay High Court denounced the "scapegoating" of

Tablighis for the pandemic. "It is now time to repent this action and take positive steps to repair the damage" (Gokhale and Modak 2020). In June 2021, the National Broadcasting Standards Authority reprimanded and fined three television stations for the tone, tenor, disrespect, and prejudice used when discussing the Tablighis and their role in spreading COVID in India (Gokhale and Modak 2021).

Despite later evidence of the Tablighis' innocence with respect to the pandemic, no official apologies were issued by government officials or the network television stations that participated in the communal rhetoric. In fact, several months later, large gatherings, both political and religious in nature, would be held throughout India amid a worsening global outbreak. Until March 2021, India had mostly escaped the worst of the pandemic. However, with upcoming legislative assembly elections in several states, political parties began holding large rallies with minimal distancing and masking throughout the spring. During the first weeks of April, millions of Hindu devotees also gathered in Haridwar for the Kumbh Mela festival. Around three thousand devotees tested positive, with many more cases likely undetected and many not following quarantine procedures (Pandey 2021). Within weeks, India's cases had skyrocketed and the country faced an unprecedented crisis in its hospitals as the medical system teetered on collapse. Tens of thousands died during the spring months as the Delta variant of COVID left India ravaged.

The pandemic rhetoric and response followed a familiar communal tone. Prior to the official arrival of COVID in India, New Delhi had faced some of the worst Hindu–Muslim riots in decades. Tensions had escalated following protests that began in December 2019 after India passed the Citizenship Amendment Act (CAA). The CAA provided a pathway to citizenship for Hindu, Jain, Christian, Buddhist, Parsi, and Sikh migrants from Pakistan, Afghanistan, and Bangladesh without documentation. Despite the foundation of secularism in India's constitution, the CAA was the first time in modern Indian history that religion could have been used to establish citizenship. Indian leaders justified this law by saying it gave sanctuary to persecuted religious minorities (Shah 2019). Noticeably absent from the list, however, were Muslims. Leaders of the ruling BJP claimed that Muslims could not be persecuted in Muslim-majority countries and thus do not need refuge in India.[4] Despite this statement, several minority Muslim groups are persecuted in South Asia, including Shias, especially Hazaras, in both Afghanistan and Pakistan, and Sufis, Ahmadiyyas, and Rohingya in Bangladesh. Muslims in Sri Lanka have also faced increasing persecution, as discussed in Section 5.

The passage of the CAA and the communal response to COVID were not abrupt or surprising; they were the culmination of decades of organizing by Hindu nationalist groups. Hindu nationalism has been present in India for well over a century, but it has gained increasing access to centralized power since the late 1980s through the BJP. The proximity of Hindu paramilitary organizations like the RSS to the BJP have deeply influenced the BJP's policy direction and platform.

Key Beliefs of Hindu Nationalists

To first understand why the CAA created such contention among the population, it is necessary to examine the origins of Hindu nationalism and the tensions between the minority Muslim community and the broader Hindu community. The scope of Hindu nationalism is not singular or simplistic; it is complex and dynamic. However, most members share certain principles that adhere to the tenets of Hindu nationalism and provide guidance for the movement. These shared principles are:

- Hinduism is the core of India and its history.
- Hindu culture and identity are under threat.
- Hindus were historically oppressed by minorities, including the Mughals and British.
- The primary threat to Hindu culture today comes from secularism and Muslims.
- The Hindu population is shrinking and the Muslim population is growing through coercive tactics, including conversion, "love jihad" (deceptive

---

[4] In a 2019 interview, India's home minister, Amit Shah, said that "it is not possible for them [Muslims] to be religiously persecuted" (Shah 2019) (www.news18.com/news/india/not-religiously-exploited-amit-shah-on-why-muslims-excluded-from-citizenship-bill-2349193.html).

marriages of Hindu women with Muslim men), high birth rates, and illegal migration from Bangladesh.[5]

Historical Origins of Hindu Nationalism

Independent India has been pulled in several directions by competing forces attempting to define the ethos of the country. Varshney (1993) emphasizes competing themes of secular pluralism versus Hindu nationalism. The idea of India as a tolerant and pluralistic melting pot was the narrative championed by independence leaders such as Nehru and Gandhi. This vision was supposed to be carried forth by the INC, although it frequently fell victim to the same type of communal narrative it accused others of, as demonstrated in the discussion in Section 2 of the INC's relationship with Sikhs. The theme of India as the home of Hinduism and its adherents has been put forth by varying levels of Hindu adherents, ranging from the moderate to the militant, and is the primary focus of this section.

The origins of Hindu nationalism cannot be traced to a single point in time. India envisioned as a singular nation is relatively recent, primarily emerging in the postcolonial era. India has long been defined by multiple facets of regional, geographic, and caste diversity. This diversity not only separated distinct religious groups from one another; it separated Hindus from one another as well. How Hinduism was and is practiced varies by caste, region, and family. Even self-identification as Hindu is not easily categorized. Instead, Hindus often identify themselves based upon things like dress, family, and daily practices (Verghese 2020). As well as being difficult to categorize, Hinduism is also pantheistic and thus not easily compared to other world religions, particularly Abrahamic religions. However, the British Raj–era censuses attempted to do just that by officially categorizing the country's religious groups into simplistic categories. In part, this census helped identify Hinduism as a distinctive "religious" tradition (Cohn 1987; Chatterjee 1993; Kaviraj 2010).

---

[5] See Figure 2 for breakdown of religious demographics of India per the most recent census.

Hindu nationalism has attempted to overcome these multiple dimensions of Hindu identity and merge them into a more singular vision that captures the essence of "Hinduness." Hindu unification has evolved alongside the concept of "Hindutva," which seeks not only to create a more integrated Hindu identity but also to assert the hegemony of Hinduism on the Indian subcontinent (Jaffrelot 2007). The BJP has also been able to capitalize on many of the repeated failures of the INC governments and to provide an alternative, even to those not particularly persuaded by Hindu nationalist rhetoric. Despite the diversity in Hinduism, the core of Hindutva frequently aligns with a specific type of north Indian Brahmin practices, such as vegetarianism (Appadurai 1990; Vanaik 2017). Many Hindu nationalists have called attention to the need to overcome caste divisions in order to unite against a common division and be "Hindu first" (Anderson and Jaffrelot 2018; Vanaik 2017); however, the leadership of the movement is largely upper caste.

Historical Persecution

As discussed in Section 1, all groups discussed in this Element fear their identity is being threatened by some other group. The creation of this fear has been accelerated by a carefully constructed narrative through Hindutva leadership. In the twenty-first century, this has been exacerbated through social media, particularly Twitter, Facebook, and WhatsApp. According to Anand (2016), complex history is often reduced to a clash of distinct religious cultures and is primarily ahistorical by nature. The Hindu nationalist version of history is one driven by violence and supported using selective translated quotes from Islamic texts in a revelatory mode. In this historical perspective, Muslims are seen as disloyal, violent with expansionary impulses, and engaged in demographic warfare. This view shapes the current fear of ongoing threat amid the backdrop of historical persecution.

The impact of perceived historical persecution has been critical in the formation of modern Hindutva. Like most nationalists, Hindu nationalists inform their current outlook and strategy based upon past experiences. First, they often focus on Hinduism before outsiders invaded. Although the specific historical frame of reference is not always clear, it occurs prior to the establishment of the New Delhi sultanate in 1206. They emphasize the invasion and occupation by the Mughals and the British. Hindutva advocates seek a return to the early days of Hinduism. Second, they use their historical experience as a warning. Being the majority was not enough to keep Hindus safe in the past. The minority subjugated them and destroyed their places of worship and could do it again. Hindus' historical passivity allowed other groups to conquer them. Accordingly, Hindus today must learn from the past and adopt a more aggressive approach. Third, they highlight the increasing demographic imbalance of a growing Muslim population and a diminishing Hindu population.

Elements of early Hindu nationalism developed alongside the broader anticolonial nationalist movement, particularly in the 1920s. Although Hindu nationalist movements had some associations with the nationalist independence movements, the independence movements were not centered around Hinduism. Most early INC leaders wanted to distance from Hindu mobilization efforts and promote secularism, maintain solidarity with Muslims, and prevent the creation of a separate Muslim state (Friedlander 2016). While history demonstrates that this pre-independence attempt at unity ultimately failed, it did not fail because of Hindu nationalism. In fact, Hindu nationalism as it is understood today had limited influence from the 1920s to the 1980s (Bhatt 2001).

Various organizations and texts served as inspirational precursors to the Hindu nationalist movement. Hindu groups such as Brahmo Samaj (1828) and Arya Samaj (1875) acted as revivalist Hindu organizations in the late nineteenth century. However, the goals of Arya Samaj should be separated from the modern understanding of Hindu nationalism. The founder of Arya Samaj, Dayananda Saraswati, merged ideas about the Aryan race with Hinduism (Bhatt 2001). According to Saraswati, the Aryans originated on the Tibetan plateau, then spread into uninhabited India and established the best nation in the world, which reigned until the Mahabharata war (3000 BC). The leaders of Arya Samaj were concerned with the increasing numbers of Christians in the country, as demonstrated by the 1871 census, and consequently endorsed proselytizing and the infallibility of the Vedas.

By the early twentieth century, various nationalist movements were organized throughout India. The most popular of these were the secular nationalists led by Nehru, Gandhi, and Subhas Chandra Bose and their political party, the INC. Members of the Hindu revivalist movements had become increasingly concerned about the approach of the INC and the secular nationalists. While the more moderate Hindu members continued to lobby the INC, the more ardent Hindu nationalists created the Hindu Mahasabha party in 1914 as a counter to the INC (Vaishnav 2019). In the 1920s, Hindu nationalist movements, specifically the RSS, went on to find support from the members and leadership of the Arya Samaj.

Although the Hindu nationalist movement had several key thinkers, it was not until the formation of the RSS under Keshav Hedgewar (1889–1940) that the movement had a clear realization and went beyond the immediate discussion of Indian independence. The RSS was originally an offshoot of the Mahasabha but quickly became an independent cultural organization. The writings of Vinayak Savarkar (1883–1966) helped guide the creation and goals of the RSS. When the RSS formed between 1924 and 1926, many Hindus had developed a resentment toward Gandhi and other INC nationalist leaders. The resentment centered around the INC leaders' support for the Muslim Khilafat movement, which, among broader goals, sought guaranteed representation for Muslims in an independent India. Savarkar adopted the elements of nationalism used in Europe to influence how nationalism was manifested in India. Essentially, Hinduism should be a lifestyle that unites geography, racial connection, and shared culture via Hindu (religion/culture), Hindi (language), and Hindustan (geography) (Chhibber and Verma 2018). Scholars of Hindu nationalism have been careful to point out that early Hindu nationalism did not explicitly exclude Muslims from the idea of the Hindu nation; instead they would operate within it (Bhatt 2001). The RSS, however, would evolve in its approach over the following decades and begin promoting not just Hindu-led governance but a Hindu nation-state.

It should also be noted that although the nationalist independence movement was secular by nature, it was still overwhelmingly led by Hindus and utilized Hindu religious imagery to mobilize the masses. This imagery, alongside what scholars call the Hindu "chauvinist" approach of independence leaders such as B. G. Tilak, made Muslim leaders even more concerned about the future political power of Muslims under a supposedly "secular" independent India (Whaites 1998). To be clear, the Congress umbrella made organizational space for the Muslim Khilafat movement, which also heavily relied on Muslim symbolism. However, reliance on religious imagery by both only helped delegitimize the allegedly secular credentials of the INC while also highlighting the differences between the two and the inevitability of Muslims as the perpetual minority in the shadow of Hindu dominance (Whaites 1998).

The partition of Bengal in 1905 and the communal violence of the 1910s and 1920s prompted Hindutva ideologues to define Hindu identity more clearly. Savarkar's conceptualization of Hindu identity was unlike that of his predecessors because of his politicization and militarization of Hinduism and the embrace of violence when necessary. This is in stark contrast to the *satyagraha* campaign of nonviolence led by Gandhi at the time. Savarkar fervently opposed Gandhi's strategy and instead advocated quite the opposite. Savarkar's militarized principles elucidated in the Mahasabha platform included:

- The enemy of our enemy is our friend.
- Hinduize all politics and militarize Hindudom.
- If the world is unjust, so must we be; if the world is aggressive, so must we be.
- Military strength is the key to greatness.
- Aggressive offense is key.
- Self-defense and creating fear in the enemy is necessary. (Bhatt 2001)

According to Savarkar, these principles should be ingrained in the Hindu child by an early age and later coincide with military training. Although such training was also encouraged outside of the military, Savarkar recommended Hindus join the military en masse so they were well equipped and trained in modern warfare (Bhatt 2001). Because Hindus did not practice these principles in the past, according to Savarkar, Hindus were dominated by outside forces. Militarization in the present safeguarded future Hindus from threats. Muslims, on the other hand, would never have loyalty to India because of the concept of the *ummah*, the global Muslim community. "Muslims first, Muslims last, Indians never" (Savarkar 1938).

After independence in 1947, the RSS became the primary Hindu nationalist organization, even though its influence within national politics was still limited. Membership grew via *shakhas*, or local RSS branches. Although activities varied, members of the RSS participated in daily "exercises," patriotic songs, weapons training, and volunteer activities within the community, a practice still followed at the present time. Following the horrors of partition, RSS members felt it urgent to prepare for future conflict. The threat came not only from Muslims but also from Muslim's secular allies, specifically in Congress. Radical Hindu nationalists held a particular grudge toward Mahatma Gandhi's secular philosophy and vision of a religiously plural society. Gandhi's vision ultimately resulted in his demise when former RSS member and Hindu radical Nathuram Godse assassinated him just five months after independence.[6] During his trial, Godse explained his motivations. He believed that Gandhi's philosophy had helped lead to partition and resulted in the suffering of millions (Gandhi 2006). Godse's actions led the Indian government to ban the RSS, although some elements of the Hindu nationalist movement openly admired Godse (Vaishnav 2019).

The RSS was banned two additional times after 1949. The first ban occurred during Indira Gandhi's Emergency (1975–1977), which essentially suspended Indian democracy and curtailed all opposition, including the free press (Dhar 2019). Any organization deemed a threat to law and public order, including the RSS, was banned. At this time, Madhukar Deoras, the key leader of the RSS, had shifted the organization toward more activist and disruptive tactics (Andersen and Damle 1987). Nearly thirteen thousand individuals were arrested during the Emergency, with 65 percent of them members of the RSS or Jana Sangth, a similar organization (Jaffrelot 1999). Indira Gandhi alleged the RSS was conspiring to commit violence and undermine the state (Bhatt 2001). Deoras and associated politicians, including future prime minister Atal Bihari Vajpayee, were arrested at the

---

[6] Godse's departure from the RSS is disputed. Although the RSS claims Godse left the organization in the mid-1930s, his family members and independent investigations claim he never left (Noorani 2013).

beginning of the Emergency for their ties to the organization. The government's crackdown led the RSS and similar organizations to recognize a growing threat not only from religious minorities, but from secular and progressive Hindus as well.

During the Emergency, Gandhi officially enshrined the word *secularism* into the constitution, although what secularism meant in the Indian context was never clearly defined (Acevado 2013). The Emergency was incredibly unpopular with the public and significantly hurt the popularity of Gandhi and the INC (Jaffrelot and Anil 2021). Consequently, the Emergency served as a key event that empowered the RSS and future opposition leaders. When the Emergency ended and elections were held, Gandhi and the INC emerged as the losers. The INC and the Gandhi dynasty had dominated postindependence elections, but this dominance was finally disrupted in 1977 when the Janata Party was elected. The Janata Party was not exclusively Hindu nationalists; rather it was a combination of anti–Emergency Rule parties. Nevertheless, the RSS was key to the success of the Janata Party because of its community-level mobilization against Gandhi (Bhatt 2001). Ultimately, attempts to suppress the RSS helped empower them and cemented their central role in Indian politics for the coming decades.

Once the Emergency ended, the RSS began heavily promoting the narrative of it oppression at the hands of the secular government (Sahasrabuddhe and Vajpayee 1991). Moving forward, the RSS did not seek direct power. Instead, its organizational power would be directed to the BJP, a party focused on Hindu identity that officially formed in 1980. From that point, a career with the BJP came via RSS membership. To succeed as a BJP politician, the support of the RSS was critical. The 1980s were a pivotal decade that moved Hindu nationalism from the margins to the forefront of Indian power. Through this growing power, Hindu nationalists began promoting the narrative of Hinduism under threat. The threat came from several sources, specifically secular politicians, leftists who waged insurgencies in the Naxal belt, and religious minorities, specifically Muslims, but evangelical Christians too. Communal violence between Hindus and Muslims increased dramatically compared to the previous decade (Wilkinson 2005).

Rise of the BJP

By the mid-1980s, under the new leadership of Lal Krishna Advani, the goals of the RSS and the BJP began merging. This coincided with a rise in tensions between Hindus and Muslims. At the center of the contention was the Babri Masjid in Ayodhya, a city in India's most populated state, Uttar Pradesh. Ayodhya, like most cities throughout India, had a Hindu majority and a Muslim minority. The history of the religious site was at the core of a voracious historical dispute (Pandey 1994). According to Hindus, a mosque was constructed in 1528 over an eleventh-century Hindu temple marking the birthplace of the god Rama, known as Ram Janmabhoomi. This construction occurred during the Mughal empire's expansion into the region. To Hindu nationalists, building a mosque over such an important religious site signaled a historical and ongoing conquest by Muslims (Bernback and Pollock 1996). Politicians referenced Ram Janmabhoomi more often as restoration of the temple became a central party platform.

Hindu symbolism and Ram Janmabhoomi were the primary focus for the BJP at the turn of the decade. In August 1990, the BJP made this focus the center of its political campaign with the launch of Ram Rath Yatra, a yearly Hindu chariot festival that commemorates Lord Jagannatha's annual visit to the Gundicha Mata temple in Odisha. Advani, the president of the BJP, launched a month-long rally visiting temples throughout India in a truck constructed like a chariot. The ultimate destination of the chariot, though, was not Gundicha Mata as illustrated in the Rig Veda. Instead, it was Ram Janmabhoomi. Thousands of Kar Sevaks joined Advani along the procession. The *yatra* was a seminal event that impassioned Hindus. Advani carried out several rallies each day during his chariot journey. As the procession left cities, religious skirmishes followed, killing hundreds across India during that month (Srinivas 1991). The *yatra* became one of the largest mass movements since independence (Van der Veer 1994).

Advani met resistance when entering the state of Bihar. He was arrested on the orders of Bihar's chief minister, Lalu Prasad, once the chariot crossed into the state. Throughout the procession, the ruling INC government attempted to place restrictions on the *yatra*, yet the orders were defied, resulting in sporadic violence. The arrest of Advani, like the arrest of RSS leaders during the Emergency, would be a defining moment in the modern history of Hindu nationalism. Advani's arrest mobilized Hindus and provided further evidence of the narrative of Hindu oppression. Despite Advani's arrest, Kar Sevaks continued to the mosque to erect saffron flags, which had become the symbol of Hindutva identity (Bhatt 2001).

The *yatra* occurred in the months leading up to the 1991 national elections and helped define the BJP's platform. Whereas previous references to Hindu identity by party leaders had been more covert, by 1991, the BJP had fully embraced Hindu identity and Hindutva as central aspects of its platform. The BJP manifesto for 1991 embraced nationalism, calling the BJP "the party of Nationalism" and using the slogan "Towards Ram Rajya," meaning the rule of Rama (Bharatiya Janata Party 1991).

Under Advani, the BJP put forth several Hindu identity platforms:

- Eliminating Article 370 from the constitution (which granted special status to Kashmir, India's only Muslim-majority state).
- Adopting a uniform civil code (which would eliminate Muslim personal law).
- Banning cow slaughter (cows are eaten by Christians and Muslims but are sacred animals to Hindus).
- Preserving "ancient" Indian cultural sites.
- Screening of Hindu epics on TV.
- Studying of Sanskrit (the language of the Vedas).
- Giving defense forces nuclear teeth.
- Restoring the Ram Temple.

The BJP did not win the national elections that year, but the party gained the most support it had ever earned up to that point, increasing its representation in the Lok Sabha from 35 to 120 seats (out of 545). The party did well where it ran candidates and won 20 percent of the popular vote, an 8.38 percent increase from just two years earlier (Election Commission of India 1991). This is significant compared to when the BJP first contested elections nationally in 1984 and received only 2 seats. The party's national loss was not disappointing to its leaders; instead, it pointed to the rapidly changing dynamics of Indian politics, the rejection of INC policies, and the growing power of Hindu nationalism. The BJP was victorious in local elections and controlled several state governments, including that of Uttar Pradesh, the location of the disputed Rama temple (Election Commission of India 1991). The BJP became a major party just ten years after it was created, and it had done so while centralizing Hindu identity. What happened in the next year would likely be the most important event for modern Hindu nationalism.

Destruction of the Babri Masjid

On December 6, 1992, between one hundred and fifty thousand and two hundred thousand Kar Sevaks marched to Ayodhya for a stone-laying ceremony. The ceremony quickly escalated into the complete demolition of the mosque. In response, the INC-led government under Narasimha Rao dismissed all BJP-led states and assumed control (Van der Veer 1994). The destruction of the mosque was important symbolically to the broader Muslim population. The act not only destroyed a minority religions site but it also symbolized destruction of the supposed protections guaranteed by the secular constitution. Reports of police collusion only served to further frustrate the Muslim population (Gargan 1993). The BJP-led government of Uttar Pradesh had assured no harm would occur to the mosque, yet the government and security forces did little to keep this promise. The INC's dismissal of the BJP government also reflected what many felt was an unchecked power that the INC continued to utilize to minimize opposition.

The destruction of the mosque served as a trigger for violence in areas with ongoing tensions between Hindus and Muslims, specifically Mumbai. Media images of Kar Sevaks dancing on the ruins of the mosque sparked outrage and initiated riots by the end of the day. Estimates vary, but nearly 1,000 deaths, mostly Muslims in Mumbai, occurred in the following weeks (Menon 2012). In March 1993, after the riots had quelled, Muslim militants committed the deadliest terrorist attack in modern Indian history up to that point. The attacks, carried out under the direction of criminal underworld leader Dawood Ibrahim, were said to be revenge for Ayodhya and the anti-Muslim riots. Ultimately, 257 people were killed and around 1,000 injured (Karkaria 2015). Ibrahim utilized the anger generated from the Babri Masjid and the riots to recruit local men (Vicziany 2007). Although Ibrahim was primarily motivated by financial incentives, the demolition of the Babri Masjid and the resulting riots resonated with many disaffected Muslims throughout South Asia (Vicziany 2007).

The mosque's destruction and the subsequent riots undoubtedly had a substantial impact on local and national politics. Hindus organized around what they saw as a major symbolic event signaling the mobilization of a Hindu cultural revitalization and a broader culture war. The BJP publicly abandoned some of its overtly militant Hindu stances in favor of a more subdued platform for the next election in 1996. The platform of the party appeared more inclusive and Advani was replaced by the more moderate Vajpayee. However, such moderation was mostly in name only. The BJP had not abandoned Hindutva completely; for example, the 1996 manifesto of BJP still referred to the Rama temple and Hindutva.

> Hindutva is a unifying principle which alone can preserve the unity and integrity of our nation ... On Coming to power, the BJP will facilitate the construction of a magnificent Shri Rama Mandir in Ayodhya which will be a tribute to *Bharat Mata*. This dream moves millions of people in our land; the concept of Rama lies at the core of their consciousness. (Bharatiya Janata Party 1996)

Religious Hindutva rhetoric was clearly not abandoned, and it attracted voters. At the state level, the BJP won more elections, including in the key states of Gujarat and Maharashtra. In Maharashtra, the BJP allied with the militant Hindutva organization Shiv Sena (Election Commission of India 1996). For the first time, the BJP won the majority of Lok Sabha seats in the 1996 elections. This new reign ended quickly, though, when the government lost a no-confidence vote and was replaced by the National Front coalition. In 1998, the BJP emerged victorious again with 182 seats. Within three months of the BJP being in power, the party fulfilled its promise of opposing nuclear apartheid. Between May 11 and May 13, India tested nuclear weapons near the border with Pakistan. Two weeks later, Pakistan responded with a similar test, establishing a nuclear South Asia and a drastic escalation in the already heightened regional tensions.

Hindu Nationalism in the Twenty-First Century

On December 13, 2001, the Parliament of India in New Delhi was attacked by Lashkar-e-Toiba (LeT) and Jaish-e-Mohammed (JeM), two Islamic extremist groups based in Pakistan. This attack, which killed nine Indians, triggered the next conflict with Pakistan – the first conflict between the two countries in the twenty-first century. The 2001 standoff between India and Pakistan lasted for six months as both sides increased troop presence surrounding the Line of Control. This was the second conflict since the two countries had become nuclear powers, both of which occurred under Hindu nationalist leadership. The conflict in the region was not only between countries; it was also within India. In 2002, amid the standoff in Kashmir, India experienced perhaps the worst Hindu–Muslim riots since independence in Gujarat.

Although a decade had passed since the riots, the site where the Babri Masjid stood remained an inspirational location for many Hindu devotees. Pilgrimages to Ayodhya were common well before the demolition of the Babri Masjid but increased in popularity following the destruction. On February 27, 2002, Hindu pilgrims and Kar Sevaks were traveling by train after completing their volunteer mission of rebuilding the Ram temple. As they returned to Gujarat, a mob, presumably Muslims, attacked their train at the Godhra station. The train ignited, trapping many inside and killing fifty-eight pilgrims. The attack sparked what many consider a pogrom targeting Muslims throughout Gujarat (Ghassem-Fachandi 2012).

The wide-scale and targeted violence occurred throughout the state, killing more than two thousand, mostly Muslims, and leaving more than one hundred thousand homeless (Dhattiwala and Biggs 2012). Concurrent economic boycotts and destruction targeting Muslim businesses continued after the pogrom (Ghassem-Fachandi 2012). The chief minister at the time, the future prime minister Narendra Modi, was heavily criticized for his lack of action. Many academic sources even called the 2002 riots an ethnic cleansing (Nussbaum 2009; Bobbio 2012). The United States denied a visa to Modi in 2005, citing the 1998 International Religious Freedom Act, which barred foreign leaders from entering the United States if they were responsible for severe violations of religious freedom. Modi was the first and only person banned from the United States under that law (Nussbaum 2009). Later Supreme Court investigations cleared Modi of the charges, but one hundred people were eventually convicted, including a BJP state minister (Jaffrelot 2012).

Modi became the prime minister in 2014, and he was reelected in a landslide in 2019 with the largest margins of any party in India in the twenty-first century. Once Modi became the prime minister, he began fulfilling long-standing BJP pledges. In 2014, Modi's US visa was accepted, and he went to the United States to hold a rally in New York City's Madison Square. In 2019, he joined President Donald Trump for an event entitled "Howdy Modi," which was attended by around fifty thousand (Palit 2019).

Modi also made important symbolic selections in his political appointees. He designated Hindu monk Yogi Adityanath the chief minister of Uttar Pradesh, the most populous state in India with a 20 percent Muslim population. Adityanath had close ties with the Hindutva movement due to his association with Gorakhnath Math, a monastic order that was critical in promoting the destruction of the Babri Masjid. Adityanath has a history of inflammatory statements toward Muslims, including the following:

- "If they kill one Hindu, there will be 100 that we kill ... If they take one Hindu girl away, there will be at least 100 that we will take 100 more. We will return whatever they do 100 fold, with interest."[7]
- "Muslims did no favor to India by staying here. They should have opposed partition, which led to the formation of Pakistan."[8]

The appointment of religious leaders to top political positions demonstrates an abandonment of secularist principles at the highest order and a commitment to religiously motivated exclusion. Coupled with the BJP's failure to elect any Muslim representatives in either 2014 or 2019, a clear theme was established. Although the BJP platform in both 2014 and 2019

[7] These quotes are from an undated speech uncovered in 2014; for more details, see www.washingtonpost.com/news/global-opinions/wp/2017/03/24/meet-the-militant-monk-spreading-islamophobia-in-india.

[8] Comments from Yogi Adityanath in a 2020 BBC interview (www.bbc.com/news/world-asia-india-51382414).

emphasized economic development and "One India," the bigger emphasis was on the need to build the Rama temple, stop infiltrators from Bangladesh, protect cows from slaughter, and eliminate Muslim personal law (Kim 2019).

BJP Mandate

Within the first year of the BJP's sweep to power in 2014, the party began working on its vision toward a more "Hinduized" India, although it was not explicitly labelled as such. Since Bangladesh's independence from Pakistan in 1971, there has been growing concern about the increasing Bangladeshi presence in the bordering northeastern Indian states, specifically Assam. The changing demographics of Assam meant it was becoming the second-largest Muslim state after Kashmir. This prompted the creation of the National Register of Citizens (NRC). The NRC required all residents of Assam to produce citizenship documents that demonstrated Indian ancestry prior to 1971. By 2019, a list was produced of all registered citizens in Assam. The list excluded approximately 1.9 million people living in the state of 31 million (BBC 2019a).

According to Home Minister Amit Shah, the NRC sought to "throw out infiltrators." Shah also used terms like "illegal immigrants," "intruders," and "termites" to refer to those living without documentation in India. However, many residents, especially poor migrant workers, were unable to produce such documentation. In response to this, Shah ensured those with Hindu, Sikh, Jain, and Christian names that were not on the NRC registry need not worry (Shah 2019). The home minister emphasized that the NRC does not discriminate based on religion. The CAA, passed in December 2019, made critics highly skeptical of this claim.

Following the sweeping success of the BJP coalition in May 2019, minority parties held limited power to stop or delay BJP policies. Consequently, the BJP moved quickly to act on its platform. Forty years of campaign promises quickly came to fruition. In a moment of great symbolic importance, on August 5, 2020, amid the coronavirus pandemic, Adityanath, Modi, and Shah took part in a major ceremony, laying the foundation stones for the new Rama temple where the Babri Masjid once stood.

Hindutva Moving Forward

Scholars must be careful to fully distinguish Hinduism from Hindutva. Hinduism is a religion, philosophy, and way of life whereas Hindutva is a politicized nationalist movement based on exclusionary rhetoric and policies. Hindutva actively works to "otherize" those, including Hindus, who do not share its vision for the future of India. Hindutva attempts to singularize Indian identity as overlapping with a specific type of predominately Hindi-speaking, Brahmin-informed Hinduism. Policy makers and supporters sympathetic to Hindutva view the world through a lens informed by historical myths that envision a world of good versus evil, Hindu versus Muslim, secular versus religious. This allows seemingly innocuous events, such as interreligious marriage, the consumption of beef, religious gatherings, and even television ads, to be incessantly described as evidence of the erosion of Hindu values.

As discussed in Section 1, India's recent categorical downgrade from full democracy to partial democracy by Freedom House should send strong warning signs across the globe. As Hindutva has become increasingly empowered, India's core democratic institutions, which have survived many internal and external shocks, have coincidingly weakened. This was first done through rhetoric and then through policy. Hindu nationalism poses a threat far beyond its own democratic institutions and will shape India's regional and international foreign policies.

Nationalism intensifies the differences between the in-group and out-group, which increases the likelihood of conflict (Mercer 1995; Schrock-Jacobson 2012). Intense nationalism can lead to more aggressive foreign policies that can cause one group to misinterpret the intentions of others while overestimating its own capabilities, making international conflict more likely (Walt 1996). The BJP's apparent abandonment of the no-first-use nuclear policy in its platform is one concerning example (Dalton 2019). The BJP's stance toward territorial disputes with China and Nepal have also been informed by its nationalist stance, including the clash with Nepal over the birthplace of Rama (Xavier 2020). If Hindutva leaders frame India and Pakistan as primordial enemies, this may lead to a more aggressive foreign policy toward them. The BJP's willingness to escalate tensions with Pakistan was demonstrated in 1998 and 2001, as well as in the border skirmishes of February 2019. This does not mean conflict only occurs when the BJP is in power, just that Hindutva philosophy informs the approach.

A wealth of literature has demonstrated that nationalism can create aggressive and expansionist foreign policies (Snyder 1991; Cottam and Cottam, 2001; Schrock-Jacobson 2012). This is in addition to the already exclusionary policies and targeted violence within the country. The Hindutva approach toward Pakistan, and vice versa, is potentially cataclysmic because of the nuclear weapons in both countries and the apparent willingness of both parties to consider using them. This concern is enhanced due to the ongoing democratic weakening in both countries. As Section 4 demonstrates, Pakistan's own problem with Islamic extremism and its long-term investment in Islamist organizations carrying out attacks in India may only escalate tensions between the two.

4 Islamic Nationalism in Pakistan

For many, Pakistan was not seen merely as a new Muslim state in South Asia, but as a homeland meant to save Muslim minorities threatened by a Hindu majority (Dhulipala 2015). The root of the word *Pakistan* means land of the pure in Urdu. To summarize Pakistan's complex style of nationalism in only one short section is challenging. Religious nationalism in Pakistan holds some similarities to that in its South Asia neighbors, but it also has some key differences. Christophe Jaffrelot has described Pakistan's ideology as nationalism without a nation in a country that is neither democratic or autocratic (Jaffrelot 2002). Given these complexities, how does religious nationalism in Pakistan compare to other regional cases? Like in India, much of Pakistan's religious nationalism has centered around defining a threat to identity. In the case of Pakistan, internally, this threat is not from another religion (although Hindus, Sikhs, and Christians certainly face persecution), but instead most of the energy

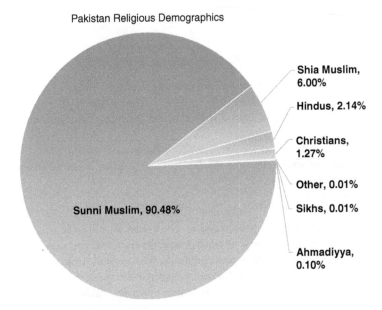

Figure 3 Pakistan Religious Demographics

is focused around defining who is a true Muslim (see Figure 3).[9] In this quest to define true Muslimhood, both the state and citizens actively persecute religious minorities, especially groups like the Ahmadiyya, which Pakistan has officially declared to be non-Muslim. The state has gone even further by punishing any Ahmadis who label themselves Muslim. Externally, the threat centers on India, which, to Pakistan, symbolizes an existential threat. This was enhanced by the Hindu nationalist belief in Akhand Bharat, an undivided India that has returned Pakistan to Bharat Mata. To understand how this type of

[9] As Figure 3 demonstrates, more than 95 percent of Pakistan is Muslim and more than 90 percent of Muslims are Sunni.

religious nationalism arose, it is important to first trace its origins and its evolution.

Key Beliefs of Islamic Nationalists in Pakistan

- Pakistan should be governed by Islamic principles.
- Ahmadis are not Muslim.
- Non-Sunni Muslims (particularly Shia and Sufis) are misguided/non-Muslim.[10]
- India is a threat and Kashmir belongs to Pakistan.
- Moderate and progressive Muslims prevent Pakistan from achieving point number one.

Creation of Pakistan

Unlike India, Pakistan was created as a homeland for a specific religious group. However, the role of Islam within the state was not clear at its origins and defining it later proved difficult. Whereas India clearly defined itself as secular and socialist, Pakistan struggled to determine if it was a state for Muslims or a state governed by Islamic principles. Pakistan's founder, Muhammad Ali Jinnah, stated that "religion or caste or creed has nothing to do with the business of the state ... all citizens are equal" (Jinnah 1947). Jinnah's death shortly after Pakistan's independence further complicated the trajectory of Pakistan's governance.

Pakistan was born out of conflict following the partition, the largest movement of humans in recorded history. The violence faced along the way by all sides undoubtedly shaped the nations they would become and how they would frame their enemies. Inevitably the image of the other side became engrained as the embodiment of everything their own side opposed. A national identity was thus built, in both India and Pakistan, along the fractured lines of partition. The identification of an enemy served as a mobilizing force for the domestic audience. The disputed territory of

[10] Many Deobandi Muslims, such as the Taliban-type groups, view Shia and Sufi as nonbelievers (*takfir*) while others, like Osama bin Laden, view them as misguided but still Muslim. There is a variation depending on which school of thought you belong to.

Kashmir, which was majority Muslim and ceded to India, aggravated these tensions.

Although Islam does not have a hierarchical structure like the rigid caste system seen in Hinduism, a social stratification still came into existence within Indian Islam (Jaffrelot 2015). This coincided with numerous other social divisions throughout South Asia, including tribal communities, converts from lower castes, and hierarchal lineages such as those seen in the Baloch and Pashtun communities. Other minority groups, including the Ahmadis as well as the Bhoras and the Hazaras, added to these complexities.

Jinnah sought to contain these ethnic divisions and believed in the ability of the *ummah* and a unitary state to override ethnic divisions. Jinnah espoused the need for "one country, one people, one religion, one language." In 1948 (Baluchistan), Jinnah reaffirmed his belief in Pakistani identity. "We are now all Pakistanis – not Baluchis, Pathans, Sindhis, Bengalis, Punjabis, and so on – and as Pakistanis we must feel, behave and act, and we should be proud to be known as Pakistanis and nothing else" (Jinnah 1948). Despite Jinnah's ambitions, Punjabi Muslims from the elite Urdu-speaking class defined Pakistani leadership and civil service from the beginning and helped exacerbate internal hostilities (Jaffrelot 2015). Ethnolinguistic divides dominated from Baluchistan to East Pakistan, now known as Bangladesh. The 1949 Constituent Assembly sought to ease some of these concerns by making Pakistan a federation, but with time it made many Bengalis feel they had limited representation. The 1952 declaration of Urdu as the official language, which was spoken by nearly no East Pakistanis, accelerated these grievances. These divides eventually led to war, a second partition, an unclear role of Islam within the state, and a continued legacy of separatism and instability.

Ethnic Separatism and the Second Partition

Geographically, the 1947 partition made minimal logistical sense. East and West Pakistan were separated by over 1,000 miles, with the entire country of India between them. The seat of power sat in Islamabad, West Pakistan (33.7 million), while the more populated East Pakistan (41.9 million) had limited political influence. Not surprisingly, the residents of East Pakistan sought weighted representation in the decision-making process and a degree of autonomy. The constitution adopted in 1956 under Ayub Khan, however, named Pakistan as an Islamic republic with powers centralized in the presidency. Khan, a Punjabi, had come to power during a 1958 coup, a governance tactic that would become all too familiar in Pakistan (Saikia 2014). The later 1962 constitution reaffirmed this centralization and nearly eliminated any mention of federalism (Jaffrelot 2015). It also gave West Pakistan authority over East Pakistan's affairs. The East Pakistan Awami League was able to capitalize on these internal frustrations and build on the concerns of what was increasingly referred to as the "two economy theory" (Iqbal 2018). The Awami League, among others, argued that Bengali goods/wealth were financing Pakistan's industrialization with minimal reinvestment in Bengal. This reaffirmed the party's desire for increased autonomy, which its members outlined in their 1966 six-point program (Ludden 2011).

The increasing popularity of the Awami League, led by Sheikh Mujibur Rahman, led to its electoral success in December 1970. The Awami League won twice as many as the next largest party, the Pakistan Peoples Party (PPP), support for which was centered in the West Pakistan provinces of Sindh and Punjab (Nohlen, Grotz, and Hartmann 2001). Yet PPP leader Zulfikar Ali Bhutto maintained that "numbers aren't everything" and that the cradle of the country was in Punjab and Sindh, not Bengal (Jaffrelot 2015: 121). Consequently, the winning party was not seated, with many West Pakistan elites saying the Awami League was covertly supported by India. This move by Bhutto led to a general strike by the Awami League and a quick escalation of hostilities.

In response to the strike by the Awami League, Pakistan initiated Operation Searchlight on March 25, 1971, and "invaded" West Pakistan, initially killing three hundred people at Dhaka University, seen as a center of resistance (Jaffrelot 2015: 122). Bengalis then attacked Urdu-speaking Biharis within the country (Jaffrelot 2015: 122). The conflict quickly led to all-out war. West Pakistan allied with Jamaat-e-Islami, a pro-Pakistani Islamist militia within Bangladesh, to carry out attacks on Hindus, intellectuals, and Awami League supporters throughout Bengal, with estimates of up to 3 million deaths, the systematic rape of two hundred thousand women, and the displacement of millions more during the eight-month conflict (Al Jazeera 2010). By November 1971, India intervened on behalf of Bangladesh, causing the war to end by December. On December 3, East Pakistan officially became Bangladesh. The country had split, and the humiliating defeat once again forced Pakistan to reckon with its identity and its style of governance. India's intervention in the conflict only helped further divide the two countries.

Cold War and Islamization Policies

Islamists never agreed with many of the ideas set forth by Jinnah. To them, Islam was not merely a cultural identifier but a guidance for law and order within the state. Organizations such as the Jamiat-e-Uleme-e-Hind (JUH) and the Jamat-e-Islami (JeI) and the philosophy of Islamic fundamentalist thinkers like Ayed Abul Maududi challenged the more progressive stances of many Pakistani elites in the leadership. Maududi, amongst others in the *ulema*, argued that Islam and Muslims could flourish only when Muslims hold power in a type of Islamic state. As Pakistan appeared to not embrace this vision, Maududi, among others in the Islamist movement, felt he could not support the state on its current path (Nasr 1996).

The 1952 Constituent Assembly made several concessions to appease the Islamists, such as declaring Pakistan an Islamic republic and shariah the supreme law (Nasr 1996). However, these declarations were not enough. Among the contentions within the Islamist community was the role of the Ahmadis. Maududi and others began publishing scathing articles targeting the Ahmadi community (Jaffrelot 2015: 451). Ahmadis were particularly targeted as blasphemous because they consider the founder, Mirza Ghulam Ahmad, the Messiah, which violates the core belief held by most Muslims that Muhammad is the final prophet (Friedmann 2003). Maududi was eventually arrested for causing communal hatred and put to death for treason (Nasr 1996). However, his beliefs continued to define and inspire Islamists throughout Pakistan and the world.

The 1956 constitution granted concessions to some of the Islamists' demands, such as requiring the president to be Muslim and not implementing laws that override the teaching of the Quran (Jaffrelot 2015). Pakistan's semi-secular aspirations remained present within the norms and institutions of Pakistan, such as the right to practice any religion without persecution. However, religious minorities still did not experience the same level of security and freedom that Muslims did. This "not secularism, not theocracy" approach simply did not go far enough for the Islamists within Pakistan. Although President Ayub Khan attempted to diminish some of their impact during his tenure (1958–1969), such as limiting certain practices like *triple talaq* and polygamy, it was not enough to stop their rising political and cultural influence.

Political leaders began noticing the growing impact of the Islamist thinkers within Pakistan, and, rather than fight against it, they sought to capitalize on it. This began with Yayha Khan (1969–1971), followed by Zulfiqar Ali Bhutto (1973–1977), and accelerated under the military regime of Zia-ul-Haq (1977–1988). Many attribute Pakistan's Islamization to Zia; however, it had been building prior to Zia's rise to power. Zulfiqar Ali Bhutto, who is often considered part of Pakistan's more progressive past, carried out several changes during his tenure. These changes included the 1973 constitution that made Islam the state religion of Pakistan. Article 260 also defined who is Muslim and not, and classified Ahmadis as non-Muslim (Nasr 1994). Additionally, in 1977, Bhutto declared *shariah* the "law of the country" and implemented some aspects of *shariah*, such as prohibition of alcohol and gambling. He also had the University Grant Commission recognize Quranic schools (Malik 1996). Bhutto likely did this to attract the more conservative voting bloc amid the growing power of Jamaat-e-Islami, which was winning a greater number of seats during the same time.

While Bhutto attempted to placate some of the conservative voting bloc's demands, it was not enough to limit the aspirations of Zia-ul-Haq. In 1977, Zia occupied perhaps the most powerful position in Pakistan as the chief of army staff. During his time, he changed the motto of the army to include faith, piety, and holy war (Fair 2014). Shortly after (July 5, 1977), he came into power via a coup that deposed and eventually executed Bhutto. Once in power, Zia accelerated the Islamization policies set forth by his predecessors. His policies also Islamized the legal, education, and bureaucratic dimensions of Pakistan (Weiss 1986). During the same time, the military also became increasingly powerful and tied to the religious right within the country. In 1984, amid allegations of voting irregularities and in order to gain legitimacy, Zia implemented a national referendum to ask if Pakistanis wanted to endorse a government that made the laws of Pakistan "in conformity with the injunctions of Islam." The vote was 98.5 percent in favor, although as Jaffrelot points out, a no to Islam was unthinkable. But the vote helped cement Pakistan's movement toward an Islamized state (Jaffrelot 2015).

These changes within Pakistan occurred alongside a rapidly transforming global and regional dynamic. Not only were tensions rising between the United States and the USSR, but the proxy war between the two was taking place in neighboring Afghanistan. Zia's policies sought to counter both Soviet and Iranian Shia influence within Afghanistan. To this end, with the help of the United States, Zia empowered radical Sunni Islamist elements within Pakistan, especially in regions bordering Afghanistan (Coll 2004). Not surprisingly, this accelerated sectarianism between Sunnis and Shias within Pakistan (and Afghanistan), which had previously been minimal (Grare 2007). Sunnis felt threatened by the newly empowered Shia state in Iran and the influence it may have both within Afghanistan and regionally.

Regional Islamist elements had had contact with one another prior to the Soviet invasion of Afghanistan. As early as 1974, Pakistan was allegedly financially supporting Afghan nationals fighting against the left-leaning regime in Kabul (Gul 2010). However, the 1979 invasion of Afghanistan by the Soviets and the Indian military expansion in Kashmir mobilized Islamist elements in Pakistan. The Pakistani intelligence agency ISI and Zia began systematically supporting *mujahideen* fighters. The growing number of Afghan refugees in the border city of Peshawar also provided a ripe recruitment pool for training soldiers to cross the border and fight. Islamists from all over the world, with estimates of thirty-five thousand or more, began descending on Pakistan as part of a broader movement to fight in an ideological and tactical battles against the Soviets (Rashid 2010). Pakistan began receiving substantial foreign aid from the United States and Saudi Arabia to train these *mujahideen* fighters (Coll 2004). While it effectively helped weaken the Soviets, it also helped empower radical Islamists in the region.

The war in Afghanistan also massively expanded the growth of *deeni madaris*, (religious seminaries) throughout Pakistan. The *deeni madaris* attracted tens of thousands of radical students from across the world who wanted to fight the Soviets in Afghanistan and later the Indians in Kashmir. These madrassas mostly taught very conservative schools of thought, such as Deobandi, and generally encouraged violent engagement with enemies as a religious duty. Once the Soviets left Afghanistan, the power vacuum left in the region allowed former *mujahideen* fighters to rise to power as part of the Taliban. Relatively porous borders between Pakistan and Afghanistan meant fighters freely flowed between the two countries. Pakistan also continued to provide ideological and logistical support to the Taliban during this time (Jaffrelot 2015).

When Zia-ul-Haq mysteriously died in a plane crash in 1988, allegedly caused by exploding mangoes, the government returned to civilian power under Benazir Bhutto, the daughter of Zulfiqar Ali Bhutto. Many believed that Bhutto and the nominally progressive PPP could moderate the increasingly conservative drift of Pakistan's government that had happened under Zia. Although Bhutto and the PPP were more progressive in their ideologies than her predecessor, her regime sprovided support for the Taliban (Rubin 2002). Bhutto also heavily invested in Islamist fighters in Kashmir, particularly the Hizb ul Mujahideen.

Bhutto's successor, Nawaz Sharif, took this legacy of support for Islamists even further (Desmond 1995). Sharif was appointed chief minister of Punjab in 1985 by Zia and worked with his Islami Jomhuri Ittihad (IJI) coalition to continue much of Zia's legacy while also challenging the progressive policies of the PPP (Jaffrelot 2015). Despite the multiple electoral contestations and power shifts between Bhutto and Sharif during the late 1980s and most of the 1990s, the military and the ISI continued to call most of the shots.

Rise of the Taliban

Pakistan's support of the Taliban was not necessarily ideological. It was a means of challenging the alliance between Afghanistan and India, exerting influence in the region, and "fixing" the separatist problems within Pakistan (Rubin 2002; Jaffrelot 2015). Some have even called the relationship between Pakistan and the Taliban a "protectorate state" (Dorronsoro 2005). India and Afghanistan were historical allies, especially since the installation of the 1979 Soviet-backed government in Kabul. India's relationship with Afghanistan declined as the Taliban came to power in 1996, with India refusing to acknowledge the Taliban's members as the leaders of the country (Paliwal 2017). Pakistan used this opportunity to further influence Afghan affairs, even though it meant supporting a radical Deobandi-inspired Islamic regime that denied even the most basic rights, such as education, to women.

Pakistan's support of the Taliban led to the empowerment of a similar extremist ideology within Pakistan itself. This helped counter India not only in Afghanistan but also in Kashmir. Following the Soviet invasion, many *mujahadeen* fighters were looking for new opportunities. Kashmir became the ideological centerpiece for the new holy war against India. Pakistan provided logistical support and sanctuary to the Hizbul Mujahadeen (the fighting wing of Jamaat-e-Islami) and to the secular Jammu and Kashmir Liberation Front (Varshney 1991). Both organizations infiltrated Kashmir, carried out terrorist attacks in the region, and engaged in battles with the Indian military.

As Pakistan experienced political turmoil throughout the 1990s, the number of radical madrassas continued to expand. Sectarianism was also on the rise, amplifying divisions between Sunnis and Shias. The Deobandi school of thought adopted by the Taliban was growing among Pakistani organizations including Lashkar-e-Jhangvi (LeJ), its parent organization, Sipah-e-Sahaba Pakistan (SSP), JeM, Har-kat-ul-Jihad-al-Islami (HUJI), and most so-called Pakistani Taliban groups (Fazil 2012). These groups thrived within Pakistani madrassas and viewed Shias, Ahmadis, and those who didn't follow their version of Islam as *takfirs*, nonbelievers. Talib fighters continued to freely cross the border between Pakistan and Afghanistan throughout the 1990s and developed well-established bases in both countries (Coll 2004). Pakistan even gave the Taliban $30 million in aid in 1997–1998 (Jaffrelot 2015). However, this relationship faltered over time, particularly with the Taliban's refusal to recognize the international border, known as the Durand Line, between the two countries (Ghufran 2009).

During the same era, the military continued to diminish the civilian power of the prime minister and the parliament through Pakistan's presidency. The power of the president, who closely aligns with the military, had increased under the eighth amendment in 1985. The eighth amendment gave the president the ability, among other things, to dissolve the parliament (Amin 1994). This new power ensured the more conservative Islamic bend of the military would maintain and grow its influence over the civilian government. In 1995, with the support of Islamists, Major General Zahirul Islam Abbasi led a failed coup against Prime Minister Benazir Bhutto (Jaffrelot 2015). In 1999, a successful military coup against Prime Minister Nawaz Sharif led to the appointment of army chief Pervez Musharraf as the new president of Pakistan (Rizvi 2000). The 1999 coup was the third in Pakistan's short history and demonstrated the limited power of civilians within the country and the growing power of the military. The coup also revealed concerning close cooperation with jihadists in both Afghanistan and Pakistan. This history of instability and Islamic extremism would soon bring the world's focus to the region.

Post-2001 Rise of Islamism

Much of the Western world knew little about Afghanistan, or even Islam, prior to 9/11. Following the 9/11 attacks, the world's attention shifted to the two pivotal countries, Afghanistan and Pakistan. Although none of the 9/11 attackers came from Afghanistan, they had all received training in in the country under the Taliban (Haass 2021). Pakistan quickly became a key US ally despite its history of support for the Taliban and regional Islamist militants.

Despite Pakistan's questionable historical ties to radical Islamic elements within its own country and Afghanistan, the United States forged a close relationship with Pakistan during the newly minted global war on terror. After the 9/11 attacks, the United States needed Pakistan's strategic support. The partnership between Pakistan and the United States had flourished during the 1980s amid the Soviet–Afghan war, and the United States returned to its Cold War partner. The United States required Pakistan to commit to several items, including stopping logistical support for Bin Laden and al-Qaeda operatives, providing US flight landing rights, sharing intelligence, and territorial access for US counterterrorism missions (Kean and Hamilton 2004).

Although there were major internal disagreements, Pakistan agreed to the US demands for the partnership and was rewarded generously by the United States and the international community. Musharraf attempted to publicly demonstrate his commitment to the global war on terror and a moderate version of Islam by banning the LeJ, requiring registration of *dini madaris* and all foreign students, and vowing to expand the educational curriculum of madrassas (Jaffrelot 2015). However, the United States remained doubtful about Musharraf's commitment to his proclaimed moderate stance (Jaffrelot 2015). Musharraf's background, including his close historical ties to Zia and Islamists, made the United States question the regime – rightfully so, as multiple reports have confirmed that Pakistan forces were helping Taliban leaders again as early as 2003, with the ISI even allegedly having ties to attacks on member states of the North Atlantic Treaty Organization (Giustozzi 2008, 2009).

Following the 2001 fall of the Taliban amid the US invasion, the Taliban, al-Qaeda, and associated forces mostly retreated to Pakistan, particularly in Waziristan in the federally administered tribal areas (FATA). While there, the Islamists grew in strength and power and were mostly left alone by the Pakistani military. This gave the Islamists de facto control of the region, and they even proclaimed the area was an Islamic state (Abbas 2010). Under US pressure, Pakistan finally deployed troops to the region. The operations were not received well given the area's history of autonomy alongside an unwillingness by many Pakistani soldiers, especially Pashtuns, to fight against their brothers (Gul 2010). This led Pakistan to ultimately negotiate with rather than fight the Islamists in the region (Fair 2014). The United States continued to cast doubt on Pakistan's commitment to tamping down extremism and escalated its drone warfare campaign, targeting the area's key Islamist leaders. Conservative Islamist alliances, such as the Muttahida Majlis-e-Ama (MMA), also grew in power during the mid-2000s and implemented Islamization policies in tribal regions, such as a ban on dancing and music and enforced compliance to Friday prayers (Jaffrelot 2015).

By 2007, a more powerful and dangerous force known as the Tehrik-i-Taliban Pakistan (TTP), often referred to as the Pakistan Taliban, emerged. Pakistan's ongoing alliance with the United States and its recent deadly military operation to root out extremists at their Red Mosque base were two key factors in the establishment of the TTP (Sayed 2021). The TTP, which allied with both the Afghan Taliban and al-Qaeda, pledged to establish *shariah* in Pakistan and to fight both the United States and Pakistan (Sayed 2021). The TTP carried out several significant attacks, including several suicide bombings, mass killings of opposition tribal leaders, and the 2007 assassination of Benazir Bhutto at a political rally (Sayed 2021). The TTP also escalated sectarian violence by explicitly targeting Shias. The targeted violence was so severe it earned the ire of Osama bin Laden, who requested the group to instead focus their efforts toward Western and Pakistani state targets (Sayed 2021). However, the TTP refused to heed bin Laden's advice.

In the border city of Quetta, this refusal culminated in ongoing targeted violence toward the Hazara ethnic group concentrated there. The Hazara are a predominantly Shia ethnic minority group that make up 0.004 percent of the population of Pakistan yet have faced incredibly high levels of violence (Human Rights Watch 2014). Many Hazara came as refugees from Afghanistan, fleeing the Taliban and other Sunni militant groups. Despite an attempt to escape persecution in Afghanistan, the Hazara people faced similar levels of violence in Pakistan. Although they are only 0.05–1 percent of the total Shia population, in 2013, nearly half of Shia killed in Pakistan were Hazaras (Human Rights Watch 2014). Multiple deadly attacks hit Hazara mosques during religious holidays and busloads of pilgrims en route to Shia holy sites. Many of these attacks specifically targeted Shia communities and facilities. The TTP isolated itself from other Islamist groups in the region by attacking an army-run school in Peshawar in 2014, killing 150 people, 134 of which were children (Jaffrelot 2015).

By the time of the school attack, Pakistan had been rapidly falling out of favor with the United States due to the relationships it maintained with certain Islamist groups, specifically the Taliban. Perhaps most damning were the allegations that Pakistan was aware of the presence of Osama bin Laden within the country and did nothing, although Pakistan heavily disputes this (Tharoor 2015). In 2011, the United States acted on intelligence that Osama bin Laden was living in a compound in Abbotabad, Pakistan, and killed him. The United States did this without notifying Pakistan for fear he would be notified internally and leave (Tharoor 2015). Around the same time, levels of sectarian violence soared to new heights. In 2013 alone, 850 Shias were killed in targeted attacks (Human Rights Watch 2014). Sectarian attacks began to decrease by 2016 following heightened attacks from 2007 onward. However, it was not an end to the violence. Harassment and attacks on religious minorities continued with minimal intervention by the state.

There was some hope for moderation with the election of Imran Khan as prime minister and his Pakistan Tehreek-e-Insaf (PTI) party in 2018. The PTI platform is the creation of an egalitarian Islamic welfare state and an end to religious discrimination in Pakistan. However, since Khan's election, the state has continued to embrace a more central role for conservative Islam. For example, in 2021, the Pakistani government established the Rehmatul-lil-Alameen Authority (RAA), a government religious body whose stated role, according to Khan, is to "inculcate moral and ethical values in the young generation" by "guarding against immoral alien cultures" (Alvi 2021). The religious body, whose chief patron is also Khan, will monitor school syllabi and "blasphemous" content in the media and in schools (DW 2021). Khan's central role on a religious committee that ensures schools' compliance with a specific version of Islam demonstrates a close relationship between the state and Islam. Critics of the new religious body cite its establishment as evidence that the state is growing more conservative and exclusionary.

These concerns escalated following Khan's comments on the Taliban's 2021 return to power in Afghanistan. Following the US withdrawal, Khan stated that the Taliban had broken "the shackles of slavery" (Press Trust of India 2021a). Khan's later remarks continued to encourage the world to support the new Taliban government. As of this writing, it is not yet clear how Pakistan's continued support for the new Taliban regime will develop. However, what is clear is that Pakistan is no longer attempting to hide its relationship with conservative Muslim elements within and outside the country. In October 2021, Khan demonstrated his decreased willingness to challenge radical Islamic elements within the country when he removed the extremist group Tehrik-i-Labbaik Pakistan from the list of organizations banned from the country (Press Trust of India 2021b). The only factor that may lead the government to distance itself from religious nationalists is demands from China, Pakistan's increasingly close ally. China is particularly invested in preventing any spill-over effects of radical Islam into Xinjiang, its Muslim-majority region with a history of separatism.

Islamic Nationalism Moving Forward

Analysts often attribute the rise of state-led religious nationalism in Pakistan to Zia-al-Haq. Under Zia, Pakistan implemented several Islamization policies, specifically defining who is and is not a Muslim. However, as this section has demonstrated, the power of religious nationalism in Pakistan is more nuanced and, to some extent, has ties with each political leader in Pakistan's history. Pakistan has gone from an unclear relationship with Islam at its founding under Jinnah, to a transformation that attempts to define a true Muslim. Muslim minorities such as the Ahmadi, Shias, and Sufis have been excluded and targeted for violence. "Heretic" religious heritage shrines such as sufi shrines, Shia mosques, and Christian churches have also been victimized.

Since independence, Islamists have built and maintained a strong network throughout the country, particularly in the regions on the border with Afghanistan. The morale of Pakistani Islamists has been strengthened since the end of the US occupation of Afghanistan and the fall of the Afghan national government. Prime Minister Imran Khan's growing public embrace of Islamist elements is indicative of the popular public support for Pakistan's embrace of conservative Islam as an extension of the state.

The proximity of Pakistan's intelligence, military, and certain political officials has allowed a radical version of Islam to become empowered and state adjacent. The extent of state involvement and support for Islamist elements has varied over time both in level of support and depending on the nature of the group. Organizations that clearly sought to fight the state of Pakistan, such as the TTP, received less support from Pakistan intelligence agencies compared to more anti-India organizations that fought in Kashmir like JeM and Hizbul Mujahadeen. However, even extremist organizations such as the TTP have received some passive state support depending on how politically expedient it is for those in power.

Pakistan's passive and active embrace of Islamist elements within the country creates a concerning regional dynamic, particularly vis-à-vis India's growing Hindu nationalist movement. This may lead to increased confrontation in Kashmir between the two nuclear powers. With the return of the Taliban in neighboring Afghanistan, it has become clear that virulent religious nationalism is here to stay for the foreseeable future within the region and that religious minorities, women, and progressives will be particularly vulnerable to associated violence.

5 Buddhist Nationalism in Sri Lanka

As the coronavirus pandemic raged throughout the world in 2020, it also took a communal tone in Sri Lanka. In April 2020, Sri Lanka announced its policy of cremating all victims who had died from the coronavirus. Cremation is forbidden to Muslims, who constitute 10 percent of Sri Lanka's population, and the World Health Organization had not recommended this policy. Despite global protest, Sri Lanka cremated the remains of Muslim coronavirus victims, including babies, without consent from the families (BBC 2020a). This decision reflected not only the poor interreligious relations within Sri Lanka but also the policy of Buddhism as a guiding doctrine in Sri Lanka. The policy continued for nearly one year before the government finally allowed families to bury victims of COVID. COVID was also used to marginalize Tamil communities and allowed anti-minority policies to become institutionalized within the context of public health and safety concerns.

Like Hindu nationalism in India, Buddhist nationalism has consolidated the vision of a Buddhist nation guided through the power of the government. Unlike India, Buddhist nationalists have not consistently rallied behind a specific party. Instead, they have supported personalities and policies such as the Rajapaksa brothers. Like the RSS in India, Buddhist nationalist policies were driven by a network of powerful Buddhist monks, especially through the BBS, in the twenty-first century. Buddhist nationalism has been a defining feature of Sri Lanka since before independence. It is entrenched within Sri Lankan society, and it often escalates into violence (Gunatilleke 2018).

Like in India, identity continues to play a defining role in Sri Lanka. However, religion and ethnicity manifest differently in Sri Lanka. In India, both religion and ethnicity form around deeply entrenched regional and caste lines. In Sri Lanka, ethnicity and religion are often used interchangeably and inform one another (Smock 2008). While ethnicity and religion have been historically important in Sri Lanka, both have also undergone many transformations. Minus occasional skirmishes, the dominant ethnoreligious groups in Sri Lanka coexisted relatively peacefully prior to and during colonization (Gunatilleke 2018). However, the colonial transformation in the nineteenth and twentieth centuries developed factitious relationships along ethnic lines. Specifically, the move toward a mercantilist capitalist system, the introduction of the British education system, and British bureaucratic favoritism introduced new tensions.

The Sinhalese, approximately 75 percent of the population, are primarily Buddhists who speak Sinhala. Sri Lankan Tamils (11 percent) are primarily Hindu and speak Tamil. Indian Tamils, also Hindu, came to Sri Lanka during the colonial era and constitute 4 percent of the population. Both groups also include religious minorities such as Tamil and Sinhala Christians. Muslims (10 percent) are not as clearly defined by ethnicity and language; instead, their ethnic identity has been shaped primarily by religion (see Figure 4). Even though they mostly speak Tamil, Muslims have rejected Tamil ethnic identification and typically identify as Moor (Faslan and Vanniasinkam 2015). As Buddhist nationalism developed as a guiding ideology in Sri Lanka, it had many overlaps with the foundational beliefs of Hindu nationalism.

Key Beliefs

- Sri Lanka is historically a Buddhist state.
- Buddhism in Sri Lanka is under local and global threat.
- Minorities have historically marginalized Sinhalese Buddhists.
- Tamils, Muslims, evangelicals, and leftists threaten Sinhalese Buddhist culture.
- The Muslim and evangelical populations are growing due to conversion and high birth rates while the Buddhist population is shrinking.

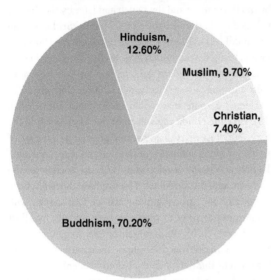

Figure 4 Sri Lanka Religious Demographics

These beliefs were formed and refined over several decades and influenced by various internal and external factors. The thirty-year civil war between the Sri Lankan state and the LTTE exacerbated these sentiments but did not cause them. Instead, Buddhist nationalist sentiment already had a strong foothold throughout Sri Lanka and was accelerated by factitious colonial policies. Elite Buddhist clergy, specifically those based in the central city of Kandy, promulgated tensions and promoted a unitary Buddhist state that utilized violence as needed (Gunatilleke 2018). To understand how these Buddhist nationalist beliefs developed in Sri Lanka, it is critical to examine the historical growth of Buddhist nationalism, including the role of historical imagery and mythologies.

Historical Origins of Buddhist Nationalism

Colonization, first by the Portuguese and the Dutch and later by the British, posed a threat to the historical Buddhist nature of Sri Lanka. Sri Lanka had been ruled by various Buddhist kingdoms since the third century (DeVotta 2011). Aggressive evangelizing by the Dutch and the British alongside the introduction of Christian schools led to an increase in conversion to Christianity by Tamils and Sinhalese (Jayawardena 2000). Conversion to Christianity was considered a route that would create clout with British colonizers (Holt 2016). Like the Hindu revivalism of the Arya Samaj in the late nineteenth century, Buddhist revivalism became popular as a means of pushing back against the growing influence of Western culture, language, and religion. Two key organizations developed in 1862: the Society for the Propagation of Buddhism and the Buddhist Theosophical Society. Both were established to counter the growing influence of Christianity and Western ideals, but more importantly to maintain their Sinhala Buddhist religion and culture (Herath 2020). Both organizations began building schools and speaking about Buddhism throughout the country, marking the establishment of a nascent Buddhist nationalism movement.

From the 1850s onward, Sinhala-speaking Sri Lankans worried that the aggressive British policy of English language imposition in Tamil-dominated areas threatened the future of Sinhala and its speakers. The British had concentrated their English schools in the Tamil areas and employed Tamils in their bureaucracies. At the same time, missionaries were heavily active in the region. Many converted to Christianity and learned English, assuming it would give them power in the colonial authority. This helped create a type of language nationalism that later merged with Buddhist religious nationalism since most Buddhists spoke Sinhala and vice versa (Dharmadasa 1992; Roberts 2021).

Not until 1891, with the establishment of the Maha Bodhi Society and the leadership of Anagarika Dharmapala, did Buddhist nationalism become more exclusionary. The Maha Bodhi Society differed from other Buddhist nationalist organizations because it tied religion and ethnicity, including language, with belonging. The goal was no longer just to promote Buddhism and counter Christian proselytizing. Instead, it was to establish

Buddhists and the Sinhalese people as the original inhabitants of the land and everyone else as visitors or invaders (Guruge 1967). Colonial divide-and-rule policies contributed to Sinhalese Buddhists' angst. British collaboration with Muslim merchants helped establish Muslims as a powerful merchant class to the disdain of Sinhalese traders (Dewaraja 1994). Dharmapala used this growing class-based ethnic divide to deride the Muslim community, comparing them to Jews and calling them alien invaders who thrive at the expense of the Sinhalese. He spoke of historical conquests by Muslims that were responsible for the elimination of Buddhism in India and the intent to eliminate Buddhism in Sri Lanka along with destroying its historical relics (Guruge 1965, 1967).

The increasingly vitriolic language toward Muslims contributed to one of the only known anti-Muslim riots in Sri Lanka in the twentieth century. The 1915 anti-Muslim riots occurred throughout Sri Lanka and were triggered by Muslims in Gampola objecting to the Buddhist celebration of Esala Perahera passing by their mosque (Holt 2016). Many Buddhists were enraged, feeling they could not openly practice their religion in their own country despite being a majority. The two-week riot resulted in major economic loss for the Muslim community but did little damage to Muslims' overall societal standing (Tambiah 1992). Muslims would continue to be one the most successful groups in the country, a stark contrast to the highly impoverished Muslims in India.

Although the 1915 riots were primarily isolated, anti-Muslim sentiment remained engrained in the Buddhist consciousness. Nevertheless, tensions shifted away from Muslims and toward Tamils for nearly the next century. This shift was aided by the adoption of a new constitution in 1931 constructed by the colonial-led Donoughmore Commission (Holt 2016). The constitution transformed Sri Lankan democratic institutions from communal to majoritarian, meaning ethnic minorities would no longer have guaranteed representation. Because of Sri Lanka's newly emerging majoritarian political system, parties mobilized along ethnic lines, but given the demographic breakdown, minorities were unable to gain meaningful representation.

Upon independence, the Sinhalese used their majority status to pass polarizing laws preventing any meaningful opposition from minority groups. These actions created a new degree of ethnic consciousness that closely merged religion and ethnicity. This transformation ultimately triggered conflict and segregation along ethnic lines (Wilson 1988). First, the Ceylon Citizenship Act of 1948 removed citizenship for Tamils who had moved to Sri Lanka during the colonial era. This effectively made at least 5 percent of the population stateless. In 1956, Sinhala, which nearly 25 percent of the population did not speak, was made the national language. As Devotta suggests, the Sinhalese used language "as a mechanism to dominate and marginalize minorities" (Devotta 2018: 281). At the same time, the state began an internal demographic engineering program that moved Sinhalese farmers into Tamil areas in the north and east (Ranathilaka 2014). The resettlement program continued through the 2000s as an attempt to transform Tamil-majority locations, diminishing Tamil chances of electoral representation in a majoritarian system (Ranathilaka 2014).

Extremist members of the Buddhist clergy became increasingly influential in politics from the 1950s and pushed political parties to adopt exclusionary policies. During the 1970s, the Jathika Chintanaya movement, which scholars have compared to "Hindutva and Talibanist Islam," emerged and served as a foundational influence for future organizations (Nuhman 2007). According to Nuhman, the organization is ideologically anti-West/capitalist, anti-Marxist, culturally conservative, and intolerant of other ethnic and religious groups. Jathika Chintanaya helped define Buddhist nationalism in Sri Lanka in the following decades. Of key importance is the group's justification of militancy and war within Buddhism. Although Sinhalese superiority had been central to earlier Buddhist nationalist thought in Sri Lanka, Jathika Chintanaya contextualized non-Buddhists as invaders who came long after Buddhists had established a thriving civilization (DeVotta 2007). These invaders were violent and sought to destroy all the advancements Buddhists had made. Violence was necessary to counter the threat.

The embedding of Sinhala Buddhist nationalism within the Sri Lankan polity created countermovements by Tamils and Muslims, although the Muslim movement was weak and mostly placated by the United National Party (UNP). Any attempt to conciliate Tamil demands, such as the 1957 Bandaranaike–Chelvanayakam Pact between Solomon Bandaranaike and

Samuel Chelvanayakam, generated backlash from Buddhist nationalists. Despite Bandaranaike's sympathy and extensive role in nurturing Sinhala Buddhist nationalism, he was assassinated by a Buddhist monk who sought to preserve his "race and religion" (Holt 2016). Tamils became second-class citizens within a decade of the implementation of Sinhala Buddhist nationalist policies. There was also an internal divide between Indian and Sri Lankan Tamils. Indian Tamils mostly worked in the central hills on tea plantations and remained incredibly poor. Sri Lankan Tamils who had benefited during the colonial era were increasingly disenfranchised and frustrated due to high unemployment and limited opportunities. The Sri Lankan Tamils were at the forefront of the resistance.

The 1970s accelerated actions limiting Tamil influence. In addition to the already diminishing electoral influence of Tamils, the Sinhalese-led government sought to reduce Tamil cultural connections. The government banned the import of Tamil-language films, Indian media, and the largest Tamil organizations in Sri Lanka. The Sinhalese presence increased across all levels of the bureaucracy. The government attempted to diminish the education and career trajectory of Tamils through university standardization policies. Tamils had historically been overrepresented in universities, especially due to historical access to the English language through missionary schools in the Tamil regions (Devotta 2000). Entry requirements for Sinhalese students were lessened while the standards for Tamils were increased (Gunawardena 1979). The national anthem symbolically was adopted only in Sinhala. The militant Tamil United Liberation Front (TULF) cited the university standardization as one of the key reasons for its demand for a separate Tamil state (Dharmadasa 1992). The lack of viable democratic options for Tamils nurtured a violent separatist movement that would dominate headlines for the next thirty years.

As Tamil militancy gained momentum via the LTTE during the 1980s and 1990s, Buddhist militant thought increased in response to Tamil militancy. Sinhalese Buddhists sought to further embed their identity within the nation through public acts of iconography, including the installation of Buddha statues and public celebration of festivals.

Civil War Era

Tamil frustration at exclusion was accelerated by the lack of willingness by police and security forces to protect Tamils and their property. This became evident to Tamils when a Sinhalese mob burned down the historic Jaffna library in 1981 (Ananthavinayagan 2020). The failure to intervene and save the nine hundred thousand books, including ancient texts, from destruction made evident to the Tamils that they were not protected under the Buddhist state apparatus. Combined with high levels of unemployment, this incident escalated dissatisfaction among the Tamils and led to the mobilization of militant Tamil organizations, particularly the LTTE. The civil war would officially begin two years later.

A key date in the transformation of Tamil and Buddhist militancy dynamics was July 1983, also known as Black July, the beginning of the Sri Lankan civil war. Black July commenced following an LTTE ambush in the Tamil city of Jaffna that killed thirteen Sinhalese Buddhist soldiers. In response, Sinhalese mobs carried out anti-Tamil pogroms throughout the country, centered in the capital city of Colombo. The estimates vary widely, but between five hundred and three thousand Tamils were killed during the pogroms (Aspinall and Regan 2013). Additionally, eight thousand Tamil homes and five thousand shops were destroyed and at least one hundred and fifty thousand people were left homeless. Many Tamils left Colombo and migrated to Tamil-majority areas in the north and east.

The LTTE quickly escalated its tactics, strategically targeting Buddhist spaces. One of the largest attacks in the early phases of the civil war occurred at one of Buddhism's holiest sites in Sri Lanka, the Jaya Sri Maha Bodhi Buddhist shrine in Anuradhapura. In 1985, the LTTE opened fire on worshippers at the shrine, killing 146 (Omer and Springs 2013). The LTTE's new strategy encouraged Buddhist nationalist sentiment among both the lay population and the clergy. Two years later, the LTTE carried out the Aranthalawa Massacre, attacking a bus with Buddhist monks and killing 37 (Omer and Springs 2013). In 1998, another large attack took place at the site of the Temple of the Tooth in Kandy, another one of Buddhism's holiest locations in Sri Lanka. The LTTE attacked the temple entrance with a truck bomb, killing 17 and injuring at least 25 (Ramasubramanian 2004).

These attacks consolidated the belief among many Buddhists that their religion was under attack and would fuel the Buddhist nationalist movement.

Buddhist Political Organizations

In addition to ideological support for Buddhist nationalism, Buddhist political parties also became popular at the height of the civil war in the 1990s and 2000s. Sinhala Veera Vidhana (SVV), Sinhala Urumaya (SU), and Jathika Hela Urumaya (JHU) were launched by Buddhist monks to increase direct Buddhist involvement in the state. At the core of the movement was an underlying fear of a country under siege by the minorities. The organizations voiced concerns about an alleged increase in forcible conversions carried out by Christian missionaries, specifically evangelicals, in addition to the increasing influence of Muslims from the Persian Gulf (Holt 2016). The organizations ran monks as political candidates and focused on turning Sri Lanka into a Buddhist state governed by Buddhist principles. Gangodawila Soma of JHU became a particularly central figure as one of the earliest monks to voice concern about what he considered a growing Muslim presence built upon historical Buddhist holy sites (Holt 2016).

The organizations were marginally successful in achieving political representation for monks, but they did not win on a national level. However, the institutionalization of monks, and the *sangha* more generally, into the political system marked a transformation in the role of Buddhism in the state (Holt 2016). The monks also utilized their influence to support specific candidates, notably the Rajapaksa brothers. In 2005, members of JHU vocally supported the campaign of Mahinda Rajapaksa, even though he was not running on an explicitly Buddhist nationalist platform. Buddhist nationalists supported Rajapaksa because of his willingness to pursue escalatory military actions toward the Tamils in an effort to end the conflict (Holt 2016). Rajapaksa won the 2005 election, as did nine JHU Buddhist monks. As promised, Rajapaksa escalated and ended the war (Eelam War IV, 2006–2009) with the Tamils during his term.

Militant Buddhist support for Rajapaksa further engrained Buddhist iconography into the nation, specifically during the war. Public patriotic exercises mixed with Buddhist religious rituals such as the *bodhi puja* became common during Eelam War IV (Weerawardhana 2017). These efforts aimed to define Sri Lanka as a Buddhist state and to clearly define the patriot and enemy along ethno-religious lines.

In 2009, the civil war came to a violent end after nearly thirty years. President Rajapaksa and his brother Gotabaya Rajapaksa, the defence secretary, utilized a strong offensive front to counter the LTTE in the north and east. The secretary-general of the United Nations reported that as many as 40,000 Tamil noncombatants may have been killed in the final phases of Eelam War IV. Other human rights organizations put the number at between 70,000 and 140,000 (Lalwani 2017). The Rajapaksa government claimed 8,649 civilians officially died during the final phases of the war. An investigative team from the United Nations Human Rights Commission (UNHRC) found evidence that both the LTTE and the government had committed war crimes, including forced disappearances, murders of civilians, and sexual violence (OHCHR 2015). With the death of the LTTE leader, Velupillai Prabhakaran, the Tamil movement in Sri Lanka was effectively finished. Buddhist nationalism, however, did not die with it; instead, it shifted focus.

Twenty-First-Century Buddhist Nationalism

To many Buddhists, Rajapaksa was a hero for helping end the Sri Lankan civil war. His support was especially high among vocal Buddhist militants. To Buddhist militants and their supporters, the defeat of the LTTE was a step toward a Buddhist nation. Rajapaksa was able to use his popularity to limit internal and international criticisms of Sri Lanka's conduct during the final stages of the war. The UN recommended Sri Lanka establish a probe into the government's conduct during the war and create truth and reconciliation committees. Although the Rajapaksa government created a timeline in 2012 to establish an inquiry, in March 2014, the United Nations said no such progress had been made (OHCHR 2015). Organizations like Human Rights Watch claim acts of genocide took place during the final phases of the war (Human Rights Watch 2010). In 2014, the UNHRC formally began an international investigation into war crimes under the Rajapaksa regime. This "Western-led" investigation angered many in Sri Lanka who saw the Rajapaksas and other high-ranking officials as heroes. Even political opponent President Maithripala Sirisena, who beat Rajapaksa in the 2015 election, claimed, "I will not allow anyone in the world to touch Jagath Jayasuriya or any other military chief or any war hero in this country" (Al Jazeera 2017). A former Rajapaksa cabinet member, Sirisena ran on a platform pledging to investigate war crimes internally, but he had to placate the Buddhist nationalist base in the name of internal sovereignty.

Once the war ended and the LTTE had been essentially obliterated, external observers hoped Sri Lanka would begin to recover and experience greater ethnic harmony. However, within three years, the creation of the BBS made clear this would not be the case. Instead, the Buddhist nature of the Sinhalese nationalist movement was more heavily emphasized. The BBS was founded by a monk, Gnansara Thero, who helped transform Buddhist nationalist rhetoric into concrete action. The narrow theological interpretation and worldview of the BBS shared many similarities with the RSS in India. The BBS leaders invited the RSS leaders (and vice versa) to learn their organizational strategies (Schontal and Walton 2016). The BBS leaders also met with Buddhist nationalist extremists in Myanmar (Schontal and Walton 2016).

In the post–civil war context, Buddhist nationalists focused on building a Buddhist state rather than interreligious coalitions. This meant targeting symbolic representations of religious minorities. In 2011, a three-hundred-year-old Muslim shrine in Anuradhapura was destroyed by a mob led by a Buddhist monk. With folkloric rationale similar to the Babri Masjid, Buddhist leaders argued the shrine was built on Buddhist land (Haviland 2011). In 2012, a mosque in Dambulla, also considered to be on sacred Buddhist land, was attacked by a Buddhist mob. D. M. Jayaratne, who served as both prime minister and head of the Ministry of Buddhism and religious affairs at the time, ordered the mosque relocated (Gunatilleke, 2018). Destruction of Hindu and Muslim sites alongside Sinhalese resettlement in Tamil-majority areas has accelerated since the end of the civil war (Devotta 2018).

By mid-2012, the BBS launched its anti-Muslim campaign. The BBS claimed Muslim cultural practices negatively impact the Sinhalese public (Nuhman 2016). According to the BBS, one prominent example of the harms of Muslim culture in Sri Lanka was halal certification. Buddhists oppose halal meat slaughter, saying it is immoral (Yusoff and Sarjoon 2017). Consequently, the BBS campaigned to eliminate halal certification of meat even though meat consumption is more widespread among Buddhists in Sri Lanka. The BBS also campaigned against the proliferation of Islamic apparel, specifically the *hijab* and the *niqab*, saying its presence is indicative of rejection of Sri Lankan culture. Finally, the BBS opposed the building and financing of new mosques, specifically those with alleged links to Gulf countries, claiming they have links to extremism (Malji 2019).

Shortly after the launch of the BBS campaign, Muslim holy sites, including mosques in Anuradhapura, Dambulla, Mahyangana, Grandpass, and Maligawatha, were targeted (Sarjoon and Hussin 2016). Propaganda was utilized to spread anti-Muslim rumors online, particularly on Facebook and Whatsapp (Sarjoon and Hussin 2016). In 2014, riots between Sinhalese and Muslim residents broke out in several towns in southwest Sri Lanka, killing four and displacing ten thousand. The most serious incidents occurred in Aluthgama and Dharga Town. Nearly all the victims who lost property and lives were Muslims (Karunarathne 2014).

Communal tensions appeared to temporarily decrease following Rajapaksa's surprising defeat in the 2015 election. Sirisena, a former minister of health in the Rajapaksa cabinet, defected from the party and ran on a platform of abolishing the executive presidency, addressing corruption, and launching a domestic inquiry into war crimes by the Rajapaksa government during the civil war (Weerawardhana 2017). The platform was a drastic shift from Rajapaksa's policies and led many Sri Lankans to believe a new era of communal harmony may be on the horizon. Unfortunately, that hope was short-lived and campaign promises were unmet. The Sirisena government faced many difficulties and, by 2017, violence spiked once again, followed by a constitutional crisis in 2018. Maintaining peace with the Buddhist nationalists was critical, and it appeared Sirisena could not placate them.

In 2018, anti-Muslim riots erupted for the first time during Sirisena's presidency. Two key events prompted the widespread violence that eventually led to a national lockdown and social media ban. First, Sinhalese patrons of a restaurant in Ampara claimed the Muslim owner had put *wandapethi*, sterilization pills, in their food. The owner, who spoke Tamil, nodded his head when asked in Sinhalese if he had contaminated the food (Borham and Attanayake 2018). Four days later, a Sinhalese taxi driver in Kandy was assaulted by Muslim youths and later died of his injuries (Borham and Attanayake 2018). Violence erupted throughout Kandy and Ampara. Buddhist mobs destroyed multiple Muslim businesses and mosques, prompting the state to institute a state of emergency and deploy national forces. The state of emergency included a ban of WhatsApp, Twitter, Facebook, and Instagram, all social media platforms where inflammatory content, including the video of the alleged meal, spread virally (Lastnamel 2018).

The 2018 riots supposedly served as a watershed moment to recruit disaffected youth into National Tawheed Jamaat (NTJ), an Islamic extremist organization led by Zahran Hashim in Sri Lanka (Amarasingam 2019). One year later, Sri Lanka would experience the deadliest attacks in its post–civil war history. On Easter 2019, almost exactly ten years since the end of the Sri Lankan civil war, the post-conflict dynamics of Sri Lanka changed dramatically. The NTJ carried out eight suicide attacks on churches, luxury hotels, and housing complexes in which a total of 259 people died. Although Buddhists were not the primary target, Buddhist nationalist mobs retaliated against Muslims over the next two months (Dibbert 2019).

The Easter attacks and the subsequent anti-Muslim attacks occurred within the shadow of the upcoming November 2019 presidential election. The attacks undoubtedly shaped the post-conflict landscape. Within a week of the Easter attacks, Gotabaya Rajapaksa, brother of former president Mahinda Rajapaksa, announced he would run for the presidency. Gotabaya previously served as his brother's secretary of defense during the civil war. Rajapaksa's hawkish history appealed to those who feared future terrorist attacks. However, no group supported the Rajapaksa candidacy more than Buddhist nationalists. Comments from Gotabaya such as "It is the monks who protect our country, religion and race" have made clear where his loyalties are (Rajapaksa 2013).

The nationalists knew that a Gotabaya Rajapaksa presidency meant Buddhist nationalist policies would be adopted. The Sinhalese Catholic population, the primary target of the attack, also supported his candidacy.

Throughout the election, Rajapaksa referenced the Easter attacks and campaigned alongside nationalist monks proclaiming he was the only one who could restore security. His Catholic wife and close relationship with the cardinal in Colombo helped secure votes from the Catholic population. Not surprising, in November 2019, Rajapaksa won the election and dominated in the Sinhalese districts while he performed poorly in Tamil- and Muslim-dominant areas (Foizee 2019). A year later, Mahinda Rajapaksa became the prime minister, cementing the family's dynastic legacy and challenging the growing democratic norms in Sri Lanka. After Gotabaya Rajapaksa's successful election, the leader of the BBS proclaimed: "We built an ideology that the country needs a Sinhala leader who does not bend down in front of minorities, now that ideology has won" (Schmall 2019).

Once the Rajapaksas were in power, the influence of Buddhist monks also increased, with monks added to government positions, including the Task Force on Archaeological Management in the eastern Tamil- and Muslim-dominated areas of Sri Lanka (Balachandran 2020). The task force was created to identify archeologically important sites that should be preserved and managed, which likely means identifying and protecting historical Buddhist sites at the cost of Islamic ones. The move shares many parallels to the historical situation in Ayodhya with the Babri Masjid and is part of a broader trend of monks' involvement in government identification of historical Buddhist sites that require relocating Muslim sites.

Buddhist Nationalism Moving Forward

Ethnicity and religion have increasingly overlapped for the past two hundred years in Sri Lanka. This has especially been influenced by the thirty-year civil war between Sri Lanka and the Tamils. To Buddhist nationalists, minority groups stand between them and fulfilling their vision of a Buddhist state. Buddhist nationalism in Sri Lanka, though, is about much more than Buddhism. Instead, it is about a civilizational home for Sinhalese Buddhists. Whereas Muslims, Christians, and Hindus have religious homes around the world, Sinhalese Buddhists only have Sri Lanka. The Buddhist nationalist vision of Sri Lanka is one where Buddhism is central not only to identity but also to governance. In a Buddhist-governed state, monks influence and dictate state policies, especially on social issues. Muslims and

Buddhists primarily had cordial relations for the past two hundred years. From independence until 2009, the enemy was primarily constructed as LTTE sympathizers. However, the second decade of the twenty-first century has focused more closely on Muslim villainization, especially against the backdrop of global Islamic extremism and the rise of groups like ISIS.

The parallels between Buddhist nationalism and Hindu nationalism are also striking. Both Buddhists and Hindus are a substantial majority within their country but position themselves as a global minority under threat from the local population in conjunction with a broader global conspiracy. Looking at the overall Muslim population in the world, Hindus in India and Buddhists in Sri Lanka see their groups as threatened. Hindu and Buddhist nationalists believe Muslims are plotting to slowly dominate their countries. Finally, although the case of Myanmar is not explored in this Element, it provides a stark warning to the world about the potential dangers of Buddhist nationalism aligning closely with the state. Buddhist nationalists in Myanmar did not consider the Rohingya, a Muslim minority, to rightfully belong in their country. This led state and nationalist militias to join forces and ethnically cleanse Rohingya areas in 2017. This targeted violence was not sudden or unexpected; instead, it escalated over several decades, beginning with a gradual erosion of Rohingya freedom and rights. The violence toward the Rohingya increased substantially as Buddhist nationalist groups like the Ma Ba Tha and the 969 movement gained prominence. The BBS has been inspired by the tactics these groups use and has even met with them in Sri Lanka and in Myanmar. Sri Lanka still has substantially more democratic features compared to Myanmar, which is currently led by a military junta. However, Sri Lanka's increased authoritarianism and striking similarities to Myanmar's Buddhist nationalist groups is cause for concern.

6 Conclusion

Symbolic Identity Galvanized around Religion

Nationalism remains an important defining force in the twenty-first century. As long as religious nationalism continues to be electorally successful in democracies and upholds power in authoritarian countries, elites will continue to utilize it as a strategy and potentially erode delicate democratic institutions. Elites will continue to signal to their in-groups that their religious identities are under threat by minorities. Discriminatory actions toward Muslims by Hindus and Buddhists through violence and legislation may also contribute to Islamic radicalism in the region and ultimately provide a feedback effect that justifies the religious nationalists' tactics. As discussed in Section 5, the NTJ utilized the 2015 anti-Muslim riots in Sri Lanka as a recruitment tool. This organization ultimately carried out the worst terrorist attack in Sri Lanka since the end of the civil war, said to be inspired by previous anti-Muslim riots (Amarasingam 2019). As discussed in Section 3, images of the destroyed Babri Masjid and acts of violence targeting Muslims in India have been used as recruitment mechanisms by Islamic extremist organizations throughout the world such as LeT and JeM (Tankel 2011).

Nationalist groups generally fear subjugation or suppression of their religious identity and exploit these fears in the population by emphasizing ahistorical accounts of a violent past by the minority in question (Anand 2016). These fears are often informed by what Kaldor (2004) calls "backward-looking" nationalism, because each group seeks a return to some mythical ahistorical point before it was negatively impacted by some external threat. In India, this fear was shaped by the historical conquest of the Mughals and the British Empire. Exploitation by the British Empire during the colonial era also informs the fears of Buddhists. In Sri Lanka, the British Empire imported minorities to work at all levels of the economic ladder, from agriculture to bureaucracy. The demographic shift led the majority Sinhalese Buddhists to feel as if they were treated as minorities within their own countries. The economic success of the Muslim traders who arrived in Sri Lanka by the seventh century also served as a source of contention for the Buddhists (Holt 2016). In Pakistan, nationalists have struggled to define the role of Islam within the state and compete with one another to create and uphold the purest version of Islam, with many looking back to the time of the prophet in the seventh century. Islamic nationalists in Pakistan want to distance themselves from the more progressive roots of Pakistan's founder, Muhammad Ali Jinnah.

Because of the emphasis on historical persecution and subjugation, religious nationalists devote abundant attention to historical architecture and symbolism (Malji 2021). As discussed in Section 2, Sikhs considered the governmental assault on the Golden Temple during OBS a pivotal moment in the escalation of the Sikh insurgency in Punjab. The destruction of holy sites by the Indian government enraged even the most moderate Sikhs. A significant portion of Section 3 addressed the impact of the Babri Masjid on the modern Hindu nationalist movement. According to Hindus, the Babri Masjid was built over an ancient temple at the birthplace of the Hindu god Rama. Although the architectural history of the site is disputed, the presence of the mosque in that location represents the historical conquest of the Mughals and their contempt toward Hindu history and culture, which is why Hindu religious volunteers, Kar Sevaks, eventually destroyed the mosque in 1992. Section 4 covered how Ahmadi and Shia mosques are frequent targets of sectarian violence in Pakistan. Violent clashes between the state and religious nationalists in Pakistan have also taken place at religious sites such as the Lal Masjid (Red Mosque) in Islamabad. Sufi shrines as well as the holy sites of other religious minorities such as Christians, Sikhs, and Hindus are also frequently targeted. Finally, as explored in Section 5, Buddhist nationalists in Sri Lanka accuse Hindus and Muslims of attempting to diminish the influence of Buddhism through their construction of mosques, temples, madrassas, and cultural centers (Gunatilleke 2015). This has even led radical Buddhists to destroy Hindu and Muslim worship sites. Buddhist nationalists have also created archaeological councils that seek to determine the historical legitimacy of non-Buddhist religious sites, particularly in Hindu- and Muslim-dominated areas.

Electoral Politics

Nationalist organizations such as the RSS in India and the BBS in Sri Lanka have been able to merge with or greatly influence political parties, guiding their policy platforms. The RSS acts as a pathway into politics for those seeking a future in the BJP. One RSS member informed the author that a career in the BJP is impossible without first going through the RSS. In India, the BJP utilizes Hindu nationalist rhetoric and policies to attract the large number of Hindu voters. Given that Hindus make up nearly 80 percent of the voting pool, it is not necessary for the BJP to attract non-Hindu voters. Consequently, utilizing Hindu nationalist rhetoric has been electorally successful. Once in power, the Hindu nationalists have passed marginalizing policies against Muslim Indians that attempt to limit their agency, such as the CAA and the NRC. While these policies marginalize Muslims, they mobilize Hindu voters who live in fear of a growing minority.

In Sri Lanka, Buddhist nationalism has long been tied to various non-state groups and smaller political parties that ran monks as candidates. Since the early 2000s, the Buddhist nationalist movement has grown close to the Rajapaksa family; the BBS even had President Mahinda Rajapaksa sign a memorandum of understanding with the group, which consolidated Buddhist nationalist support behind him. The Rajapaksas and their political party frequently engage in communal language while giving speeches on the campaign trail. Although Buddhist nationalist organizations like the BBS have not acted as a pathway into politics in the same way as the RSS, they nevertheless greatly influence the trajectory and policy positions of leading political parties.

Finally, in Pakistan, various Islamist organizations have held uncomfortably close proximity to the military and civilian leadership and consequently have significant political influence. This has been seen in the increasing influence of Islam in the state's institutions and constitution. Radical Islamic elements such as the Jama'at-e Islami have successfully run for local office and have also formed ruling coalitions with larger parties. Even progressive parties such as the PPP have supported Islamist parties, including the Taliban, in order to advance their political goals. Both progressive and conservative political parties have passed laws that marginalize minority populations, specifically the Ahmadi. Nevertheless, Islam continues to play an increasingly large role within the government and across political parties.

Final Thoughts

Religious nationalism is only one of the many threats facing the twenty-first century. As these sections have demonstrated, the characteristics of religious nationalism are complex and interconnected. While religious nationalism is not inherently violent, in South Asia, it has been closely linked to violence. This Element has demonstrated that religious nationalism in

South Asia has been growing for decades with some constant characteristics alongside new dynamics. There is evidence of growing resistance to nationalist policies in India, where some of the largest protests in its history took place following the passage of the CAA in 2019. Such resistance demonstrated a potential growing population opposed to the nationalist policies of the government. The trajectory and impact of these protests is not yet clear. Similar large-scale protests have not recently occurred in Sri Lanka or Pakistan.

All three countries continue to be tinderboxes that may escalate into violence at any moment. When religious nationalism is combined with centralized power, it weakens the rule of law and human rights, especially for religious minorities. The empowerment of nationalist parties not only threatens local and regional stability, but global stability. However, just as groups and leaders have the power to mobilize violence and division, they also have the power to mobilize unity and peace. As Jawaharlal Nehru, the first prime minister of India, said, "The only alternative to coexistence is codestruction."

Abbreviations

ACJU:	All Ceylon Jamiyyathul Ulama
ASEAN:	Association of Southeast Asian Nations
BBS:	Bodu Bala Sena
BJP:	Bharatiya Jana Party
CAA:	Citizenship Amendment Act
HUJI:	Har-kat-ul-Jihad-al-Islami
HUM:	Harkat-ul-Mujahideen
INC:	Indian National Congress
JeI:	Jamaat-e-Islami Pakistan
JeM:	Jaish-e-Mohammad
LeJ:	Lashkar-e-Jhangvi
LeT:	Lashkar-e-Toiba
LOC:	Line of Control
LTTE:	Liberation Tamil Tigers Elam
NRC:	National Register of Citizens
NTJ:	National Tawheed Jamaat
OBS:	Operation Blue Star
RSS:	Rashtriya Swayamsevak Sangh
SAARC:	South Asia Association for Regional Cooperation
SLORC:	State Law and Order Restoration Council
SSP:	Sipah e Sahaba Pakistan
TULF:	Tamil United Liberation Front
UNP:	United National Party

Terms

Akhand Bharat: Hindu nationalist vision of undivided India from Afghanistan to Burma

Arya Samaj: A nineteenth-century Hindu reform movement

Babri Masjid: Mosque in Ayodhya torn down by Hindu Nationalists due to the belief it was built on top of an ancient Hindu temple representing the birthplace of Ram

Bharat Mata: Mother India; Hindu goddess

Bodhi Puja: A Buddhist religious ceremony seeking blessings from the Bodhi tree where the Buddha achieved enlightenment

Bodhisattva: A person on the bath toward attaining Buddhahood

Brahmo Samaj: A nineteenth-century Hindu reform movement

Damdani Taksal: Sikh Educational Organization

Deeni Madari: Islamic Seminaries in Pakistan

Dharam Yudh Morcha: A Sikh civil resistance agitation movement

Esala Perahera: Sri Lankan Buddhist festival of the Tooth

Guru Granth Sahib: Religious scripture of Sikhism

Kar Sevaks: Religious volunteers or devotees usually associated with Hindu nationalism

Kara: Steel bangle worn by Sikhs

Kirpan: Sword carried by Sikhs

Lok Sabha: Indian parliament

Misls: Sovereign Sikh states common during the eighteenth century

Morchas: Nonviolent demonstration, usually against the government, wherein participants gather and often court arrest

Mujahideen: Muslim fighters; frequently referenced in the Afghanistan conflict

Nanakpanthis: Mystical Sikh community that follows the practices of Guru Nanak

Ram Janmabhoomi: Site believed to be the birthplace of the god Rama

Ram Rath Yatra: Political/religious rally led by the BJP in 1990

Rashtriya Swayamsevak Sangh: Hindu militant organization founded in 1925 in India

Sangha: Buddhist community

Sarkar-a-Khalsa: Sikh Empire

Satyagraha: Nonviolent tactic of resistance adopted by Gandhi

Shakhas: Local RSS branches

Triple Talaq: Form of Islamic divorce enacted by repeating "I divorce thee" three times

Ulema: Body of Muslim scholars

Ummah: Global Muslim community

References

Abbas, H. 2010. An Assessment of Pakistan's Peace Agreements with Militants in Waziristan (2004–2008). In *The Afghanistan–Pakistan Theater: Militant Islam, Security & Stability*, edited by D. Gartenstein-Ross and C. D. May (pp. 7–17). Foundation for Defense of Democracies.

Acevado, D. 2013. Secularism in the Indian Context. *Law and Social Inquiry* 38(1): 138–167.

Al Jazeera. 2010. Bangladesh Sets Up War Crimes Court. https://bit.ly/3xOb2hG.

Al Jazeera. 2017. Sri Lanka Leader to Shield General from War Crimes Case. https://bit.ly/3QBC7xf.

Alvi, M. 2021. Imran Khan Announces Rehmatul-lil-Alameen Authority. *International News*. https://bit.ly/3HG99IC.

Amarasingham, A. 2019. Terrorism on the Teardrop Island: Understanding the Easter 2019 Attacks in Sri Lanka. *CTC Sentinel* 12(5): 1–10.

Amin, T. 1994. Pakistan in 1993: Some Dramatic Changes. *Asian Survey* 34(2): 191–199.

Anand, D. 2016. *Hindu Nationalism in India and the Politics of Fear*. Springer.

Ananthavinayagan, T. 2020. The Burning of Jaffna Public Library: Sri Lanka's First Step toward Civil War. *The Diplomat*. https://bit.ly/3OBsmNT.

Andersen, W., and S. Damle. 1987. *Brotherhood in Saffron: A Study of Hindu Revivalism*. Westview.

Anderson, B. 2006. *Imagined Communities: Reflections on the Origin and Spread of Nationalism*. Verso.

Anderson, E., and C. Jaffrelot. 2018. Hindu Nationalism and the "Saffronisation of the Public Sphere": An interview with Christophe Jaffrelot. *Contemporary South Asia* 26(4): 468–482.

Appadurai, A. 1990. Disjuncture and Difference in the Global Cultural Economy. *Theory, Culture & Society* 7(2–3): 295–310.

Armstrong, J. 1997. Religious Nationalism and Collective Violence. *Nations and Nationalism* 3(4): 597–606.

Aspinall, E., R. Jeffrey, and A. J. Regan, eds. 2013. *Diminishing Conflicts in Asia and the Pacific: Why Some Subside and Others Don't.* Routledge.

Atwal, P. 2021. *Royals and Rebels: The Rise and Fall of the Sikh Empire.* Oxford University Press.

Bal, H. 2019. How the Congress Propped up Bhindranwale. *Caravan.* caravanmagazine.in/conflict/how-the-congress-propped-up-bhindranwale.

Bal, H. 2020. Why Delhi Police Did Nothing to Stop Attacks on Muslims. *New York Times.* www.nytimes.com/2020/03/03/opinion/delhi-pogrom.html.

Balachandran, P. K. 2020. Why the Presidential Task Force on Archaeology in Eastern Province Has No Muslim or Tamil? *Sri Lanka Brief.* https://bit.ly/3OAszR9.

BBC. 2019a. Assam NRC: What's Next for 1.9 Million "Stateless" Indians? www.bbc.com/news/world-asia-india-49520593.

BBC. 2019b. Why a Special Law on Kashmir Is Controversial. www.bbc.com/news/world-asia-india-40897522.

BBC. 2020a. Coronavirus Funerals: Sri Lanka's Muslims Decry Forced Cremation. www.bbc.com/news/world-asia-53295551.

BBC. 2020b. Kashmir: India Uses "Draconian" Law to Extend House Arrest of Former Chief Ministers. www.bbc.com/news/world-asia-india-51410380.

Beachler, D. 2007. The Politics of Genocide Scholarship: The Case of Bangladesh. *Patterns of Prejudice* 41(5): 467–492.

Bernbeck, R., and S. Pollock. 1996. Ayodhya, Archaeology and Identity. *Current Anthropology* 37: 133–42.

Betigeri, A. 2014. How India's Subsidized Farms Have Created a Water Crisis. Public Radio International. https://bit.ly/3Oynkl0.

Bharatiya Janata Party. 1991. *Towards Ram Rajya. Mid-Term Poll to Lok Sabha, May 1991: Our Commitments*. Bharatiya Janata Party.

Bharatiya Janata Party. 1996. *For a Strong and Prosperous India: Election Manifesto*. Bharatiya Janata Party.

Bhatt, C. 2001. *Hindu Nationalism: Origins, Ideologies, and Modern Myths*. Berg.

Bianchini, S., S. Chaturvedi, R. Ivekovic, and R. Samaddar. 2004. *Partitions: Reshaping States and Minds*. Routledge.

Bizman, A., and Y. Yinon. 2001. Intergroup and Interpersonal Threats As Determinants of Prejudice: The Moderating Role of In-Group Identification. *Basic and Applied Social Psychology* 23(3): 191–196.

Björklund, F. 2006. The East European "Ethnic Nation": Myth or Reality? *European Journal of Political Research* 45(1): 93–121.

Bloom, P. B. N., G. Arikan, and M. Courtemanche. 2015. Religious Social Identity, Religious Belief, and Anti-immigration Sentiment. *American Political Science Review* 109(2): 203–221.

Bobbio, T. 2012. Making Gujarat Vibrant: Hindutva, Development and the Rise of Subnationalism in India. *Third World Quarterly* 33(4): 657–672.

Borham, M., and D. Attanayake. 2018. Tension in Ampara after Fake "Sterilization Pills" Controversy. *Sunday Observer*. https://bit.ly/3y7nOJE.

Central Intelligence Agency. 2000. *Punjab Military Conflict*. Central Intelligence Agency.

Chandra, B., M. Mukherjee, A. Mukherjee, K. N. Panikkar, and S. Mahajan. 2016. *India's Struggle for Independence*. Penguin UK.

Chatterjee, P. 1993. *The Nation and Its Fragments: Colonial and Postcolonial Histories*. Princeton University Press.

Chhibber, P., and R. Verma. 2018. *Ideology and Identity: The Changing Party Systems of India*. Cambridge University Press.

Chima, J. 1997. Why Some Ethnic Insurgencies Decline: Political Parties and Social Cleavages in Punjab and Northern Ireland Compared. *Journal of Commonwealth & Comparative Politics* 35(3): 1–26. https://doi.org/10.1080/14662049708447750.

Chima, J. 2008. *The Sikh Separatist Insurgency in India: Political Leadership and Ethnonationalist Movements*. Sage.

Cohn, B. 1987. The Census, Social Structure and Objectification in South Asia. In *An Anthropologist among the Historians and Other Essays*, edited by B. Cohn (pp. 224–254). Oxford University Press.

Coll, S. 2004. *Ghost Wars: The Secret History of the CIA, Afghanistan, and Bin Laden, from the Soviet Invasion to September 10, 2001*. Penguin.

Committee for the Protection of Journalists (CPJ). 2021. Number of Journalists behind Bars Reaches Global High. https://bit.ly/3xFEJBA

Corsi, M. 2006. Communalism and the Green Revolution in Punjab. *Journal of Developing Societies* 22(2): 85–109.

Cottam, M. L., and R. W. Cottam. 2001. *Nationalism & Politics: The Political Behavior of Nation States*. Lynne Rienner.

Dalton, T. 2019. *Much Ado about India's No First Use Policy*. Carnegie Endowment for International Peace.

De Silva, C. 2011. A Hydraulic Civilization. *The Sri Lanka Reader: History, Culture, Politics*, edited by J. Holt (pp. 53–57). Duke University Press.

Desmond, E. 1995. The Insurgency in Kashmir (1989–1991). *Contemporary South Asia* 4(1): 5–16.

Devotta, N. 2000. Control Democracy, Institutional Decay, and the Quest for Eelam: Explaining Ethnic Conflict in Sri Lanka. *Pacific Affairs* 73(1): 55–76. https://doi.org/10.2307/2672284.

Devotta, N. 2007. Sinhalese Buddhist Nationalist Ideology: Implications for Politics and Conflict Resolution in Sri Lanka. *East West Center Policy Studies* 40: 1–50.

DeVotta, N. 2011. Sri Lanka: From Turmoil to Dynasty. *Journal of Democracy* 22(2): 130–144.

Devotta, N. 2018. Religious Intolerance in Post–Civil War Sri Lanka. *Asian Affairs* 49(2): 278–300.

Dewaraja, L. S. 1994. *The Muslims of Sri Lanka: One Thousand Years of Ethnic Harmony, 900–1915.* Lanka Islamic Foundation.

Dhanagare, D. N. 1988. The Green Revolution and Social Inequalities in Rural India. *Bulletin of Concerned Asian Scholars* 20(2): 2–13. https://doi.org/10.1080/14672715.1988.10404444.

Dhar, P. N. 2019. *Indira Gandhi, the "Emergency" and Indian Democracy.* Oxford University Press.

Dharmadasa, K. 1992. *Language, Religion, and Ethnic Assertiveness: The Growth of Sinhalese Nationalism in Sri Lanka.* University of Michigan Press.

Dhattiwala, R., and M. Biggs. 2012. The Political Logic of Ethnic Violence: The Anti-Muslim Pogrom in Gujarat 2002. *Politics & Society* 40(4): 483–516.

Dhavan, P. 2011. *When Sparrows Became Hawks: The Making of the Sikh Warrior Tradition, 1699–1799.* Oxford University Press.

Dhillon, G. 1974. Evolution of the Demand for a Sikh Homeland. *Indian Journal of Political Science* 35(4): 362–373.

Dhoss, M. C. 2014. Repainting Religious Landscape: Economics of Conversion and Making of Rice Christians in Colonial South India (1781–1880). *Studies in History* 30(2): 179–200. https://doi.org/10.1177/0257643014534370.

Dhulipala, V. 2015. *Creating a New Medina.* Cambridge University Press.

Dibbert, T. 2019. Buddhist Anger Could Tear Sri Lanka Apart. *Foreign Policy.* https://bit.ly/3Of0I9B.

Diez-Medrano, J. 2005. Nation, Citizenship and Immigration in Contemporary Spain. *International Journal on Multicultural Societies* 7(2): 133–156.

Dorronsoro, G. 2005. *Revolution Unending: Afghanistan 1979 to the Present.* Columbia University Press.

DW. 2021. Pakistan: New Religious Body Draws Ire from Rights Activists. www.dw.com/en/pakistan-new-religious-body-draws-ire-from-rights-activists/a-59518865

Election Commission of India. 1991. www.elections.in/parliamentary-constituencies/1991-election-results.html.

Election Commission of India. 1996. General (11th Lok Sabha) Election Results India. www.elections.in/parliamentary-constituencies/1996-election-results.html.

Esses, V. M., J. F. Dovidio, L. M. Jackson, and T. L. Armstrong. 2001. The Immigration Dilemma: The Role of Perceived Group Competition, Ethnic Prejudice, and National Identity. *Journal of Social Issues* 57(3): 389–412.

Fair, C. 2006. Diaspora Involvement in Insurgencies: Insights from the Khalistan and Tamil Eelam Movements. *Nationalism and Ethnic Politics* 11(1): 125–156. https://doi.org/10.1080/13537110590927845.

Fair, C. 2014. *Fighting to the End: The Pakistan Army's Way of War*. Oxford University Press.

Faslan, M., and N. Vanniasinkam. 2015. *Fracturing Community: Intra-group Relations among the Muslims of Sri Lanka*. International Centre for Ethnic Studies.

Fazil, S. 2012. *Sectarianism and Conflict: The View from Pakistan*. Danish Institute for International Studies.

Fenech, L. E. 2001. Martyrdom and the Execution of Guru Arjan in Early Sikh Sources. *Journal of the American Oriental Society*: 20–31.

Foizee, B. 2019. Sri Lanka's Election Results Reveal a Divided Country. *The Diplomat*. https://bit.ly/3HIpdJK.

Freedom House. 2021a. Freedom in the World 2021: India. https://freedomhouse.org/country/india/freedom-world/2021.

Freedom House. 2021b. Freedom in the World 2021: Pakistan. https://freedomhouse.org/country/pakistan/freedom-world/2021.

Freedom House. 2021c. Freedom in the World 2021: Sri Lanka. https://freedomhouse.org/country/srilanka/freedom-world/2021.

Friedland, R. 2001. Religious Nationalism and the Problem of Collective Representation. *Annual Review of Sociology* 27(1): 125–152.

Friedlander, P. 2016. Hinduism and Politics. In *The Routledge Handbook of Religion and Politics*, edited by J. Haynes (pp. 70–71). Routledge.

Friedmann, Y. 2003. *Tolerance and Coercion in Islam: Interfaith Relations in the Muslim Tradition*. Cambridge University Press.

Gandhi, R. 2006. *Gandhi: The Man, His People, and the Empire*. University of California Press.

Gargan, E. 1993. Trust Is Torn: Police Role in Bombay Riots. *New York Times* 31:1.

Gellner, E. 2008. *Nations and Nationalism*. Cornell University Press.

Ghassem-Fachandi, P. 2012. *Pogrom in Gujarat*. Princeton University Press.

Ghufran, N., 2009. Pushtun Ethnonationalism and the Taliban Insurgency in the North West Frontier Province of Pakistan. *Asian Survey* 49(6): 1092–1114.

Gill, S. S., and K. C. Singhal. 1984. Farmers' Agitation: Response to Development Crisis of Agriculture. *Economic and Political Weekly* 19(40): 1728–1732.

Giustozzi, A. 2008. *Koran, Kalashnikov, and Laptop*. Columbia University Press.

Giustozzi, A. 2009. *Decoding the New Taliban: Insights from the Afghan Field*. Hurst.

Gokhale, O., and S. Modak. 2020. Bombay HC Slams Govt: Tabligh Is a Scapegoat to Warn Muslims; Fix Damage. *Indian Express*. August 2. https://indianexpress.com/article/india/tablighi-jamaat-case-firs-bombay-hc-coronavirus-6565460.

Gorski, P. S., and G. Türkmen-Dervişoğlu. 2013. Religion, Nationalism, and Violence: An Integrated Approach. *Annual Review of Sociology* 39: 193–210.

Grare, F. 2007. The Evolution of Sectarian Conflicts in Pakistan and the Ever-Changing Face of Islamic Violence. *South Asia: Journal of South Asian Studies* 30(1): 127–143.

Greenfeld, L. 1996. The Modern Religion? *Critical Review* 10(2): 169–191.

Grewal, J. S. 1998. *The Sikhs of the Punjab*. The New Cambridge History of India. Cambridge University Press.

Grzymala-Busse, A. 2019. Religious Nationalism and Religious Influence. In *Oxford Research Encyclopedia of Politics*, edited by W. Thompson. Oxford University Press. https://doi.org/10.1093/acrefore/9780190228637 .013.813.

Gul, I. 2010. *The Most Dangerous Place: Pakistan's Lawless Frontier*. Penguin UK.

Gunatilleke, G. 2018. *The Chronic and the Entrenched: Ethno-religious Violence in Sri Lanka*. International Centre for Ethnic Studies.

Gunawardena, C. 1979. Ethnic Representation, Regional Imbalance and University Admissions in Sri Lanka. *Comparative Education* 15(3): 301–312.

Guruge, A. 1965. *Return to Righteousness: A Collection of Speeches, Essays and Letters of Anagarika Dharmapala*. Government Press.

Guruge, A. 1967. *Anagarika Dharmapala*. Department of Cultural Affairs.

Haass, R. 2021. The World 9/11 Made. Council on Foreign Relations. www.cfr.org/article/world-911-made.

Haggard, S., and R. Kaufman. 2021. *Backsliding: Democratic Regress in the Contemporary World*. Elements in Political Economy. Cambridge University Press. https://doi.org/10.1017/9781108957809.

Hastings, A. 1997. *The Construction of Nationhood: Ethnicity, Religion and Nationalism*. Cambridge University Press.

Haviland, C. 2011. Sri Lanka Buddhist Monks Destroy Muslim Shrine. BBC. www.bbc.com/news/world-south-asia-14926002.

Hayes, C. J. H. 1960. *Nationalism: A Religion*. Macmillan.

Herath, D. 2020. Constructing Buddhists in Sri Lanka and Myanmar: Imaginary of a Historically Victimised Community. *Asian Studies Review* 44(2): 315–334.

Hindustan Times. 2022. India Still "Partly Free" in Freedom House Report. https://bit.ly/3QPOvKi.

Holt, J. C. 2016. *Buddhist Extremists and Muslim Minorities: Religious Conflict in Contemporary Sri Lanka*. Oxford University Press.

Hroch, M. 1985. *Social Preconditions of National Revival in Europe*. Cambridge University Press.

Human Rights Watch. 2010. Sri Lanka: New Evidence of Wartime Abuses. www.hrw.org/news/2010/05/20/sri-lanka-new-evidence-wartime-abuses.

Human Rights Watch. 2014. Pakistan: Rampant Killings of Shia by Extremists. June 29. www.hrw.org/news/2014/06/29/pakistan-ram pant-killings-shia-extremists.

Human Rights Watch. 2020. Discrimination against Muslims under India's New Citizenship Policy. https://bit.ly/3OCU5xL

Indian Express. 2020. Say Sorry. December 17. https://bit.ly/3OsybwS.

Iqbal, I. 2018. State of (the) Mind: The Bengali Intellectual Milieu and Envisioning the State in the Post-colonial Era. *South Asia: Journal of South Asian Studies* 41(4): 876–891.

Israelsen, S., and A. Malji. 2021. COVID-19 in India: A Comparative Analysis of the Kerala and Gujarat Development Models' Initial Responses. *Progress in Development Studies* 21(4): 397–418.

Jaffrelot, C. 1999. *The Hindu Nationalist Movement and Indian Politics: 1925 to the 1990s: Strategies of Identity-Building, Implantation and Mobilisation (With Special Reference to Central India)*. Penguin Books India.

Jaffrelot, C, ed. 2002. *Pakistan: Nationalism without a Nation*. Zed Books.

Jaffrelot, C. 2007. *Hindu Nationalism: A Reader*. Princeton University Press.

Jaffrelot, C. 2012. Gujarat 2002: What Justice for the Victims? The Supreme Court, the SIT, the Police and the State Judiciary. *Economic and Political Weekly* 47(8): 77–89.

Jaffrelot, C. 2015. *The Pakistan Paradox: Instability and Resilience*. Oxford University Press.

Jaffrelot, C., and P. Anil. 2021. Interpreting the Emergency. *Heidelberg Papers in South Asian and Comparative Politics* (79): 1–18.

Jalal, A. 1998. Nation, Reason and Religion: Punjab's Role in the Partition of India. *Economic and Political Weekly* 33(32): 2183–2190.

Jayawardena, K. 2000. *Nobodies to Somebodies: The Rise of Colonial Bourgeoisie in Sri Lanka*. Social Scientists Association.

Jinnah, M. A. 1947. Presidential Address to the Constituent Assembly, Karachi, Pakistan. August 11.

Jinnah, M. A. 1948. Speech. Civic Address at Quetta Municipality. June 15.

Jones, F. L., and P. Smith. 2001. Individual and Societal Bases of National Identity: A Comparative Multi-level Analysis. *European Sociological Review* 17(2): 103–118.

Juergensmeyer, M. 1988. The Logic of Religious Violence: The Case of the Punjab. *Contributions to Indian Sociology* 22(1): 65–88.

Juergensmeyer, M. 1996. The Worldwide Rise of Religious Nationalism. *Journal of International Affairs* 50(1): 1–20.

Juergensmeyer, M. 2003. *Terror in the Mind of God: The Global Rise of Religious Violence*. University of California Press.

Kaldor, M. 2004. Nationalism and Globalisation. *Nations and Nationalism* 10 (1–2): 161–177.

Kang, C. S. 2005. Counterterrorism: Punjab, a Case Study. Doctoral dissertation, School of Criminology, Simon Fraser University.

Karkaria, B. 2015. How the 1993 Blasts Changed Mumbai Forever. BBC. www.bbc.com/news/world-asia-india-33713846.

Karunarathne, W. 2014. BBS on the War Path. *Sunday Leader*.

Kaviraj, S. 2010. Indian Nationalism. In *Oxford Companion to Indian Politics*, edited by N. G. Jayal and P. B. Mehta (pp. 317–322). Oxford University Press.

Kean, T., and L. Hamilton. 2004. *The 9/11 Commission Report: Final Report of the National Commission on Terrorist Attacks upon the United States*. Vol. 3. Government Printing Office.

Khalidi, O. 2001. Ethnic Group Recruitment in the Indian Army: The Contrasting Cases of Sikhs, Muslims, Gurkhas and Others. *Pacific Affairs* 74(4): 529–552. https://doi.org/10.2307/3557805.

Kim, A. 2019. The New Nationalism in Modi's India. *The Diplomat*.

Kohli, A. 1997. Can Democracies Accommodate Ethnic Nationalism? Rise and Decline of Self-Determination Movements in India. *Journal of Asian Studies* 56(2): 325–344.

Lafont, J. M. 2002. *Maharaja Ranjit Singh: Lord of the Five Rivers*. Oxford University Press.

Lahav, G. 2004. *Immigration and Politics in the New Europe: Reinventing Borders*. Cambridge University Press.

Lalwani, S. 2017. Size Still Matters: Explaining Sri Lanka's Counterinsurgency Victory over the Tamil Tigers. *Small Wars & Insurgencies* 28(1): 119–165. https://doi.org/10.1080/09592318.2016.1263470.

Lastnamel, F. 2018. Resurgence of Ethno-religious Sentiment against Muslims in Sri Lanka: Recent Anti-Muslim Violence in Ampara and Kandy. *Journal of Politics and Law* 11(4): 27–39.

Ludden, D. 2011. The Politics of Independence in Bangladesh. *Economic and Political Weekly* 79–85.

Mahmood, C. 1989. Sikh Rebellion and the Hindu Concept of Order. *Asian Survey* 29(3): 326–340. https://doi.org/10.2307/2644668.

Mahmood, C. 1996. Why Sikhs Fight. *Anthropological Contributions to Conflict Resolution* 29(11): 11–30.

Malik, J. 1996. *Colonization of Islam: Dissolution of Traditional Institutions of Learning*. Manohar.

Malji, A. 2019. Interview with BBS CEO. December 23.

Malji, A. 2021. People Don't Want a Mosque Here: Destruction of Minority Religious Sites As a Strategy of Nationalism. *Journal of Religion and Violence* 9(1): 50–69.

Malji, A., and A. Amarasingam. 2021. Forced Cremation of COVID Dead in Sri Lanka Further Marginalizes Muslim Community. *Religion Dispatches*. https://religiondispatches.org/forced-cremation-of-covid-dead-in-sri-lanka-further-marginalizes-muslim-community.

Malji, A., and S. T. Raza. 2021. The Securitization of Love Jihad. *Religions* 12: 1074.

Menon, M. 2012. *Riots and after in Mumbai: Chronicles of Truth and Reconciliation*. Sage Publications India.

Mercer, J. 1995. Anarchy and Identity. *International Organization* 49(2): 229–252.

Mittal, A. 2021. *Endless War: The Destroyed Land, Life, and Identity of the Tamil People in Sri Lanka*. Oakland Institute.

Mukherjee, U. N. 1909. *Hindus: A Dying Race*. M. Banerjee and Company.

Nasr, S. V. R. 1994. *The Vanguard of the Islamic Revolution: The Jama'at-i Islami of Pakistan*. University of California Press.

Nasr, S. V. R. 1996. *Mawdudi and the Making of Islamic Revivalism*. Oxford University Press on Demand.

New York Times. 1982. Under Threat, New Delhi Braces for Sikh Threat.

Nohlen, D., F. Grotz, and C. Hartmann, eds. 2001. *Elections in Asia and the Pacific: A Data Handbook: Volume I: Middle East, Central Asia, and South Asia*. Oxford University Press.

Noorani, A. G. 2013. The BJP and Nathuram Godse. *Frontline*. https://frontline.thehindu.com/books/the-bjp-and-nathuram-godse/article4328688.ece.

Nuhman, M. 2007. *Sri Lankan Muslims: Ethnic Identity within Cultural Diversity*. International Centre for Ethnic Studies.

Nussbaum, M. 2009. *The Clash Within: Democracy, Religious Violence, and India's Future*. Harvard University Press.

Nuhman, M. 2016. Sinhala Buddhist Nationalism and Muslim Identity in Sri Lanka. In *Buddhist Extremists and Muslim Minorities: Religious Conflict in Contemporary Sri Lanka*, edited by J. Holt (pp. 18–53). Oxford University Press.

Oberoi, H. S. 1987. From Punjab to Khalistan: Territoriality and Metacommentary. *Pacific Affairs* 60(1): 26–41.

O'Brien, C. C. 1994. *Ancestral Voices. Religion and Nationalism in Ireland*. University of Chicago Press.

OHCHR. 2015. Report of the OHCHR Investigation on Sri Lanka.

Omer, A., and J. A.Springs. 2013. *Religious Nationalism: A Reference Handbook*. ABC-CLIO.

Palit, P. S. 2019. Modi and the Indian Diaspora. *RSIS Commentaries*, no. 241. www.rsis.edu.sg/wp-content/uploads/2019/11/CO19241.pdf.

Paliwal, A. 2017. *My Enemy's Enemy: India in Afghanistan from the Soviet Invasion to the US Withdrawal*. Oxford University Press.

Pandey, G. 1994. Modes of History Writing: New Hindu History of Ayodhya. *Economic and Political Weekly* 29(5): 1523–1528.

Pandey, G. 2021. India COVID: Kumbh Mela Pilgrims Turn into Super-Spreaders. BBC. May 10. www.bbc.com/news/world-asia-india-57005563.

Pakistan Tehreek-e-Insaf. 2011. Pakistan. Web Archive. www.loc.gov/item/lcwaN0008538.

Pillalamarri, A. 2014. India's Anti-Sikh Riots, 30 Years On. *The Diplomat*.

Platteau, J. P. 2017. *Islam Instrumentalized*. Cambridge University Press.

Press Trust of India. 2020. Tablighi Members Moving like "Human Bombs": Himachal BJP Chief. *Deccan Herald*. April 4. https://bit.ly/3uj4pTV.

Press Trust of India. 2021a. "Afghans Have Broken 'Shackles' of Slavery": PM Imran Khan. August 16. www.thehindu.com/news/international/afghans-have-broken-shackles-of-slavery-pak-pm-imran-khan/article35939794.ece.

Press Trust of India. 2021b. PM Imran Khan Removes Extremist Group Tehreek-i-Labbaik Pakistan from Banned Outfits. *The Hindu*. November 7. https://bit.ly/3OyLdcf.

Purewal, S. 2012. The Evolution of the Sikh Secessionist Movement in Western Liberal Democracies. *International Journal of Business and Social Science* 3(18): 107–113.

Raghaven, S. 2005. Protecting the Raj: The Army in India and Internal Security, c. 1919–39. *Small Wars and Insurgencies* 16(3): 253–279.

Rajapaksa, G. 2013. Campaign Speech at Buddhist Brigade Training School.

Ramasubramanian, R. 2004. *Suicide Terrorism in Sri Lanka*. Institute of Peace and Conflict Studies.

Ranathilaka, M. B. 2014. Nexus between Land and Ethnic Conflict in Sri Lanka: Real or Imaginary? An Analysis of Land, Agricultural and Irrigation Policies in Sri Lanka. *Sri Lanka Journal of Economic Research* 2(2): 69–89.

Rao, M. 2011. Love Jihad and Demographic Fears. *Indian Journal of Gender Studies* 18(3): 425–430.

Rashid, A. 2010. *Taliban: Militant Islam, Oil and Fundamentalism in Central Asia*. Yale University Press.

Razavy, M. 2006. Sikh Militant Movements in Canada. *Terrorism and Political Violence* 18(1): 79–93.

Rieffer, B. A. J. 2003. Religion and Nationalism: Understanding the Consequences of a Complex Relationship. *Ethnicities* 3(2): 215–242.

Rizvi, H. A. 2000. Pakistan in 1999: Back to Square One. *Asian Survey* 40(1): 208–218.

Roberts, M. 2021. *Exploring Confrontation: Sri Lanka: Politics, Culture and History*. Routledge.

Roy, K. 2011. *War, Culture and Society in Early Modern South Asia: 1740–1849*. Routledge.

Rubin, B. R. 2002. *The Fragmentation of Afghanistan: State Formation and Collapse in the International System*. Yale University Press.

Sahasrabuddhe, P. G., and M. C. Vajpayee. 1991. *The People versus Emergency: A Saga of Struggle*. Suruchi Prakashan.

Saikia, Y. 2014. Ayub Khan and Modern Islam: Transforming Citizens and the Nation in Pakistan. *South Asia: Journal of South Asian Studies* 37(2): 292–305.

Sandhu, J. 2014. Green Revolution: A Case Study of Punjab. *Proceedings of the Indian History Congress* 75: 1192–1199.

Sarjoon, A., M. Yusoff, and N. Hussin. 2016. Anti-Muslim Sentiments and Violence: A Major Threat to Ethnic Reconciliation and Ethnic Harmony in Post-war Sri Lanka. *Religions* 7(10): 1–18.

Savarkar, V. D. 1949. *Hindu Rashtra Darsha: A Collection of the Presidential Speeches Delivered from the Hindu Mahasabha Platform*. A. S. Bhide.

Savarkar, V. D. 1938. Presidential Address, 20th Session of Akhil Bharat Hindu Mahasabha, Nagpur.

Sayed, A. 2021. The Evolution and Future of Tehrik-e-Taliban Pakistan. Carnegie Endowment for International Peace. https://bit.ly/3OyLFqX.

Schmall, E. 2019. Buddhist Nationalists Claim Victory in Sri Lankan Election. Associated Press. November 27. https://apnews.com/article/mountains-ap-top-news-reinventing-faith-weekend-reads-race-and-ethnicity-bf051a4b2673484f8460131a7500b0ec.

Schonthal, B., and M. J. Walton. 2016. The (New) Buddhist Nationalisms? Symmetries and Specificities in Sri Lanka and Myanmar. *Contemporary Buddhism* 17(1): 81–115.

Schrock-Jacobson, G. 2012. The Violent Consequences of the Nation: Nationalism and the Initiation of Interstate War. *Journal of Conflict Resolution* 56(5): 825–852.

Seiple, C. 2013. *The Routledge Handbook of Religion and Security*. Routledge.

Sen, P. 2019. Hindu Nationalists Open Self-Styled Religious Courts As a Rebuke to Sharia Law. Religion News Service. https://bit.ly/3xPi2uF.

Shah, A. 2019. Speech to the Rajya Sabha. November 20. www.ndtv.com/india-news/home-minister-amit-shah-in-parliament-nrc-will-be-carried-out-across-the-country-no-one-from-any-rel-2135590.

Shani, G. 2008. *Sikh Nationalism and Identity in a Global Age*. Routledge.

Shani, G. 2020. Midnight's Children: Religion and Nationalism in South Asia. In *Religion and Nationalism in Asia*, edited by G. Shani and T. Kibe (pp. 32–47). Routledge.

Shiromani Akali Dal. 1973. The Anandpur Sahib Resolution. SGPC. October 16–17.

Shiv Sena. 2019. Public Letter to Narendra Modi. May 1. www.tribuneindia.com/news/archive/nation/news-detail-766518.

Shoeb, R., T. A. Warriach, and M. I. Chawla. 2015. Mughal–Sikh Relations: Revisited. *Journal of the Research Society of Pakistan* 52(2): 165–181.

Singh, G. 2000. *Ethnic Conflict in India: A Case-Study of Punjab*. Palgrave Macmillan.

Singh, K. 2004. The Anandpur Sahib Resolution and Other Akali Demands. In *A History of the Sikhs 2: 1839–2004*, edited by K. Singh (pp. 337–350). Oxford University Press. https://doi.org/10.1093/acprof:oso/9780195673098.003.0020.

Singh, P. 2014. The Guru Granth Sahib. In *The Oxford Handbook of Sikh Studies*, edited by P. Singh and L. E. Fenech (pp. 125–135). Oxford University Press.

Singh, P., and J. M. Rai. 2008. *Empire of the Sikhs: The Life and Times of Maharaja Ranjit Singh*. Peter Owen.

Singh, V. B. 2004. Rise of the BJP and Decline of the Congress: An Appraisal. In *Indian Democracy: Meanings and Practicesi*, edited by R. Vora and S. Palshikar (pp. 299–324). Sage.

Smith, A. D. 1998. *Nationalism and Modernism*. Routledge.

Smith, D. 2019. *The First Anglo–Sikh War 1845–46: The Betrayal of the Khalsa*. Osprey.

Smith, M. 1991. *Burma: Insurgency and the Politics of Ethnicity*. Politics in Contemporary Asia Series. Zed Books.

Smock, D. 2008. Religion in World Affairs. Special Report. United States Institute of Peace.

Sniderman, P. M., L. Hagendoorn, and M. Prior. 2004. Predisposing Factors and Situational Triggers: Exclusionary Reactions to Immigrant Minorities. *American Political Science Review* 98(1): 35–49.

Snyder, J. 1991. *Myths of Empire: Domestic Politics and International Ambition*. Cornell University Press.

Srinivas, M. N. 1991. On Living in a Revolution. *Economic and Political Weekly* 26(13): 833–835.

Stephan, W. G., and C. W. Stephan. 1996. Predicting Prejudice. *International Journal of Intercultural Relations* 20(3–4): 409–426.

Talbot, I., and G. Singh. 2009. *The Partition of India*. Cambridge University Press.

Tambiah, S. 1992. *Buddhism Betrayed? Religion, Politics and Violence in Sri Lanka*. University of Chicago Press.

Tamir, Y. 1995. *Liberal Nationalism*. Princeton University Press.

Tankel, S. 2011. *Storming the World Stage: The Story of Lashkar e Toiba*. Oxford University Press.

Tatla, D. S. 2005. *The Sikh Diaspora: The Search for Statehood*. Routledge.

Tausch, N., M. Hewstone, and R. Roy. 2009. The Relationships between Contact, Status and Prejudice: An Integrated Threat Theory Analysis of Hindu–Muslim Relations in India. *Journal of Community & Applied Social Psychology* 19(2): 83–94.

Thampi, M. 1999. Indian Soldiers, Policeman, and Watchmen in China in the Nineteenth and Early Twentieth Centuries *China Report* 35(4): 403–437.

Tharoor, I. 2015. Pakistani Leaders Knew Osama bin Laden Was in Pakistan, Says Former Defense Minister. *Washington Post*. October 14. https://wapo.st/3xNqIlx.

Tully, M., and S. Jacob. 2006. *Amritsar: Mrs. Gandhi's Last Battle*. Rupa Press.

Udupa, S. 2018. Enterprise Hindutva and Social Media in Urban India. *Contemporary South Asia* 26(4): 453–467.

United Nations Security Council. 1998. http://unscr.com/en/resolutions/1172.

Vaishnav, M. 2019. *The BJP in Power: Indian Democracy and Religious Nationalism*. Carnegie Endowment for International Peace.

Van der Veer, P. 1994. *Religious Nationalism: Hindus and Muslims in India*. University of California Press.

Vanaik, A. 2017. *The Rise of Hindu Authoritarianism: Secular Claims, Communal Realities*. Verso.

Varshney, A. 1991. India, Pakistan, and Kashmir: Antinomies of Nationalism. *Asian Survey* 31(11): 997–1019.

Varshney, A. 1993. Contested Meanings: India's National Identity, Hindu Nationalism and the Politics of Anxiety. *Daedalus* 122(3): 227–261.

Verghese, A. 2020. Taking Other Religions Seriously: A Comparative Survey of Hindus in India. *Politics and Religion* 13(3): 1–35. https://doi.org/10.1017/s1755048320000280.

Vicziany, M. 2007. Understanding the 1993 Mumbai Bombings: Madrassas and the Hierarchy of Terror. *Journal of South Asian Studies* 30(1):43–73.

Wald, K. D., and C. Wilcox. 2006. Getting Religion: Has Political Science Rediscovered the Faith Factor? *American Political Science Review* 100(4): 523–529.

Walt, S. 1996. *Revolution and War*. Cornell University Press.

Weerawardhana, C. 2017. Paradigms of [In]Tolerance? On Sri Lanka's Bodu Bala Sena and Transformative Dynamics of Lived Religion. In *Lived Religion and the Politics of (In) Tolerance*, edited by R. Ganzevoort, N. Ammerman, and S. Sremac (pp. 19–39). Palgrave Macmillan.

Weiss, A. M. 1986. The Historical Debate on Islam and the State in South Asia. In *Islamic Reassertion in Pakistan: The Application of Islamic Laws in a Modern State*, edited by A. Weiss (pp. 1–20). Syracuse University Press.

Whaites, A. 1998. Political Cohesion in Pakistan: Jinnah and the Ideological State. *Contemporary South Asia* 7(2): 181–192.

Wijesiriwardhana, S. 2010. Purawasi Manpeth. FLICT.

Wilkinson, S. 2005. *Religious Politics and Communal Violence*. Oxford University Press.

Wilson, A. 1988. *The Break-Up of Sri Lanka: The Sinhalese–Tamil Conflict*. Orient Longman Limited.

Wolf, S. O. 2017. Pakistan and State-Sponsored Terrorism in South Asia. In *Terrorism Revisited*, edited by P. Casaca and S. O. Wolf (pp. 109–155). Springer.

Xavier, C. 2020. Interpreting the India–Nepal Border Dispute. Brookings Institute. https://brook.gs/3xQ1ra6.

Yasir, S. 2020. Gandhi's Killer Evokes Admiration As Never Before. *New York Times*. https://nyti.ms/3zY3j3u.

Yusoff, M. A., and A. Sarjoon. 2017. Anti-halal and Anti-animal Slaughtering Campaigns and Their Impact in Post-war Sri Lanka. *Religions* 8(4): 46.

Yusuf, I. 2018. Three Faces of the Rohingya Crisis: Religious Nationalism, Asian Islamophobia, and Delegitimizing Citizenship. *Studia Islamika* 25(3): 503–542.

Cambridge Elements ☰

Religion and Violence

James R. Lewis
Wuhan University

James R. Lewis is Professor at Wuhan University, and the
author and editor of a number of volumes, including *The
Cambridge Companion to Religion and Terrorism*.

Margo Kitts
Hawai'i Pacific University

Margo Kitts edits the *Journal of Religion and Violence* and is
Professor and Coordinator of Religious Studies and East-West
Classical Studies at Hawai'i Pacific University in Honolulu.

ABOUT THE SERIES

Violence motivated by religious beliefs has become all too common
in the years since the 9/11 attacks. Not surprisingly, interest in the
topic of religion and violence has grown substantially since then.
This Elements series on Religion and Violence addresses this new,
frontier topic in a series of ca. fifty individual Elements.
Collectively, the volumes will examine a range of topics, including
violence in major world religious traditions, theories of religion
and violence, holy war, witch hunting, and human sacrifice,
among others.

Cambridge Elements ≡

Religion and Violence